PRETTY WELL ADJUSTED

*An awkward young woman's hilarious journey
from poverty to the American dream*

J. Walker

*This collection of stories is dedicated to my sister, Desiree, who
after enduring a ridiculous childhood,
has been battling a relentless illness since 2001.*

*I also dedicate this to my husband, Randy,
whom I've loved deeply since I was twenty-three,
and who loves me more than a BMW.*

CONTENTS

FORWARD

People who know these stories ask me how I am normal. Well, no one is. I can't be around maggots, and cats attack me sometimes, unprovoked. I'm indifferent to popcorn ceilings, and anti-tiles that look like wood flooring. Whatever happened to ice milk and the Lyme Disease vaccine? No thank you, scobys!

I have a great life in a house on a lake with a loving husband, a creative job, and a karaoke machine. (Well, it's actually a system.) I spend hundreds of dollars a year on flowers and enjoy a good Manhattan. I couldn't ask for more.

These stories are unique, which is why I'm sharing them (with most names changed to protect us all). And they are true, to the best of my memory.

Please laugh with me at the weirdness and the pain...it made me who I am, and I am grateful.

TELEVISION DEBUT

How do you choose an outfit for your television debut in a local news story about being poor?

I was twelve and new in town. Mom had decided just three weeks earlier over Christmas break to sell all of our stuff and move the family from New York to Wyoming in search of jobs. About a week earlier, we settled into one-bedroom efficiency at the Red and White Motel in Casper, and she had gone to the unemployment office with her boyfriend.

I was finishing up my turn in the shower when my older sister knocked on the bathroom door and asked if she could come in.

"Mom brought home a TV news crew. You have to get dressed."

"What?"

"I guess they're doing a story on unemployment in Wyoming, and Mom said they could interview us. They want to talk to us kids, too."

"You're kidding me." I was excited. What a way to start a new school, famous from a TV story. On my first day, people would be wondering if I was part of the TV family and impressed that I was from New York. Mom had sold Wyoming to us kids as a place of hope, jobs, and common folk who would accept us for who we were. The kids at school would surely see me as TV-cool and one of them.

"Can you do me a favor?" I said to my sister. "Can you get me my brown Sweet-Orrs and my brown velour Sergio Valente sweater?" It was the first outfit I could think of, and it was clean. The sweater was originally a gift to Mom from my second oldest brother Derek, who was finishing out his prison term in New York. The Sweet-Orr painter pants were from a neighborhood friend in Saugerties. By 1983, both were years out of style, but I considered them one of my two best ensembles.

I emerged from the bathroom with a wet head and a fresh, brown outfit. I sat on the convertible sofa next to my two sisters and one brother. I didn't see Kenny, my eighteen-year old brother, and I didn't care that he wouldn't be on the show. He framed me for drinking the Robitussin. Mom found the brand new empty bottle on top of the refrigerator, and he accused me, even though I witnessed him drinking it.

The reporter, Ann Kelly, was sitting on a side chair with her camera crew. She had blonde hair, blue eyes, and about eight thick eyelashes on each lid.

It was good she didn't come a couple of days ago. Running low on groceries, Mom went to a food pantry at a local church and brought home some spaghetti and sauce and other non-perishables, like packets of instant oatmeal and applesauce. We cooked up the spaghetti, and it was the consistency of paste, but we ate it anyway. I ate a lot of it, and I had been generating a steady flow of noisy but seemingly odor-free church spaghetti gas.

Lying on the floor of the motel room, watching Knight Rider, I got up a couple of times to let some noise out in the bathroom, but the frequent trips were starting to look suspicious to my four siblings, and I was missing the show. That's when I formulated a plan: create an auditory diversion. I coughed loud enough to mask the sound coming out of my behind. This worked well because the strain of coughing would force out some air, until my third oldest brother Edward exposed me.

"Jeneane's trying to cover up her farts with coughing."

"I am not."

"Don't lie."

Having been wrongly convicted of the Robitussin incident, I decided to admit guilt and continue to quietly pass as much church spaghetti gas as I could without being detected. A few days earlier, Edward offered me a dollar to sniff the farts out of the motel couch. It would have been easy money, but it wasn't worth the damage to my dignity.

Now, the news crew wanted to talk to me.

"How do you feel about your parents being unemployed?" Anne Kelly asked us kids. The camera was on us.

"It's hard because we don't have enough money to do what we want," my older sister said.

I had no problem with that statement, but I did have a problem with the word "parents." Mom's boyfriend was not my parent. I had never met my dad, but I didn't like being referred to as Mom's boyfriend's daughter.

"Thank you," Ann Kelly said as her crew shut down the camera. "The story will run on Tuesday night on channel two. Best of luck to you all. I know it's hard to find a job in this economy."

"Sometimes you gotta scrape bubble gum up off the streets to make ends meet," Mom added.

"Ooo, I like that quote. Can you say it again on camera?"

"Sure."

The crew restarted the camera, and Mom repeated her statement.

"Sometimes you gotta scrape bubble gum up off the streets to make ends meet."

"That's a wrap. Thank you again. Take care, everyone."

The segment ran two days before I started school. It ended with a close-up of Mom saying, "Sometimes you gotta scrape bubble gum up off the streets to make ends meet."

I was on camera a couple of times, and I expected to be recognized by everyone at my new school. Clearly all of the seventh graders in Casper must have watched that particular news show running the segment on unemployment in Wyoming, but only one of my classmates recognized me.

"Yeah, that was me," I admitted, hoping she would spread the information.

The TV appearance did not make me popular in Casper in junior high, and neither did anything else. Eventually, the brown Sweet-Orrs ended up at the Salvation Army along with the Sergio Valente sweater, and looking back, I often wonder whether they ever made it back into show business.

WHO'S YOUR DADDY?

When I was fourteen, I got drunk at my mother's first wedding. Ron Humborg had won her heart a few months earlier by bringing her chicken nuggets during her evening shift at the gas station in Evansville, Wyoming. He drove a big, black, fancy car and looked like a mini Clint Eastwood, his hair slicked back with Groom & Clean. He whistled each time he said the "s" sound.

It was a jeans and t-shirt wedding in the backyard of Ron's parents' house in Glen Rock, Wyoming. I siphoned off two rocks' glasses worth of my mom's Gallo Chablis, and I had quite the buzz, which I really didn't know how to manage. All I knew was that Ron's father said he would be mighty proud to be my Grandpa, and Ron asked me if he could adopt me and my seven-year-old sister Helene someday. We had already been through about six potential boyfriend-dads—Richie with no T, Nick, Tom, Jerry, Lenny, and Ritchie with a T. I wasn't surprised by another strange man's dad offer.

"I guess so," I replied to Ron's request. Helene was more open to the suggestion and started calling him "Dad" right away, even though she had a dad named Tom back in New York.

Mom seemed happy that day. She was enjoying the euphoria of a new romance with Ron. She had splurged on a white blouse to wear with her jeans. Being petty chubby, I wore another pair of my mom's jeans and one of her old sweaters—bulky, blue, with thin, red horizontal stripes and a large hole in the right side.

As they said, "I do," tears came, partly because of the wine, and partly because I thought life might be different and better with a husband-dad. Mom's boyfriends usually lasted only two years or so, and this guy's parents had a decent house, which, that day, was also the scene of my third accidental penis sighting.

"Oh, woops, someone's in here," I heard a kindly voice say as I pushed open the already ajar door to the bathroom. I saw my new Grandpa's bald penis being tucked back into the fly of his jeans. Before I could be identified, I turned and ran back to the rest of the party.

"I don't know who, but someone walked in on me when I was using the bathroom," I overheard new Grandpa with the bald penis say. Up until that point, I thought penises were covered entirely with hair. I figured I'd lay low and not admit to the sighting. He really should have closed the door.

We had lived with the last guy, Ritchie with a T, for the past two years in a trailer on the prairie with no running water, cable, or phone. It was Ritchie's idea to move to Wyoming from upstate New York in search of better jobs and opportunity. A couple of weeks before the wedding, Ritchie took me for a walk outside the trailer and explained, "Your mother's moving into town with Helene and her new boyfriend. You can either live with me and I'll be your dad and support you as I've been doing for the past couple of years, or go with her." Tears welled up in his eyes.

"Okay, I'll think about it." I really didn't have to think. There was no way I was letting a man who used to put my mother in head-locks and threaten to shoot my brother Edward be my dad. And in town, we could have running water. My mom knew I wasn't happy about this new Ron guy, and she must have put Ritchie up to offering me to stay with him to punish me and be his consolation prize.

Mom was a pretty, natural blonde with big, light-blue eyes and a very fair complexion, resembling Cybill Shepherd. She was born at an orphanage in Pittsburgh, Pennsylvania, at the end of World War II, biological parents unknown. I can imagine how excited Elizabeth and Edmund, a German couple, must have been when they adopted this week-old, beautiful baby girl! Elizabeth had an adult form of muscular dystrophy and couldn't have children. They named my mom Helene, after Elizabeth's sister, the nun, and adopted a boy named William a couple of years later.

Growing up, Helene's adoptive father, Edmund, was a machinist who made a good living with his own business. Elizabeth was active in the Catholic Church, especially in the art of gossip. After a Sunday service, Helene would listen to her on the phone, judging the other parishioners. "Did you see the color of the feather in Esther Helm's hat? And the size of the pattern in Mrs. Ober's tweed? What was she thinking?" They vacationed during the summer months on the shores of Lake Erie, and took Helene to New York City to buy her the proper, fashionable clothing for a young lady.

One day, when she was about ten years old, my mother, Helene, went to the five and dime store with some pocket money and bought a pair of white tennis shoes. "What is that on your feet?" her mother, Elizabeth, yelled.

"Just tennis shoes, Mom. I like them. They were only ninety-nine cents."

"Take those off right now! No daughter of mine is going to show her face in a pair of cheap shoes! We get our clothes at designer stores!" And with that, Helene cemented her notion that her mother's materialistic beliefs were bad and to be avoided at all costs. The next several years of disobeying the rules led to her eventual legal disownment by her parents.

"Mom, Dad, this is Ken. He works with me at the hospital." Seventeen-year-old Helene had invited Ken Walker, an orderly where she was learning to nurse, to a spaghetti dinner in the basement of the Catholic Church. Their jaws dropped. The problem was, Ken was the wrong color. They made polite conversation, ate their spaghetti dinner, and went home to argue. Elizabeth and Edmund kicked Helene out of the house, and, of course, she went to live with Ken, who fathered four children with her over the next several years, out of wedlock.

After Helene had her second child, Derek, her mother died. Despite being disowned, she offered to help her father adjust to his new life, and got a surprise. The extended family blamed her for her mother's death. So in reaction, she cut them off completely, which became her routine way of dealing with strained relationships. And why wouldn't it be? She was abandoned by her birth family and her adopted family. I understand now that this is why she lost touch with my father, and I didn't meet him until I was twenty-four.

❈ ❈ ❈

One day, at about five years-old, I was home from a half-day of kindergarten in Yonkers, New York, when I asked my mom what I thought was a perfectly logical question. "Mom? Did you smoke when you were pregnant with me?"

"No," she said washing a small sandwich plate in the kitchen.

"Did you smoke when you were pregnant with Kenny?"

"Uh, yes."

"Derek?"

"I think so, yes."

"Edward?"

"Yep."

"Desiree?"

"Yes."

"Is that why they're black? From the ashes?"

She dropped the plate in the sink, shut off the water, turned, and looked down at me. I knew I had done something very wrong.

"Don't you *ever* say that again! They're *not* black. They're white, just like you."

Even at five, I knew my three older brothers and older sister were browner than I was. I had red hair and green eyes and freckles. My mom was like me. She had blonde hair and light blue eyes.

Kenny, the oldest, kind of looked like me, with medium-brown skin, green eyes, and loose, dark brown curls on his head. Derek, the second oldest, looked the most similar to Desiree, who was just older than me. They both had a light brown complexion, green eyes, and soft, wavy, almost straight brown hair. They shared a couple of features: a wider nose and large space between their two front teeth. Edward was the third oldest, and the brownest. He had dark brown eyes and thick, black, straight hair.

Now that I was in school, people were asking me questions about why my brothers and sister didn't look like me, and I wanted to know, too. "Are you adopted?" they would ask.

"No," I would say. "They just look like our dad, and I look like my mom. Plus, they're very tan."

"There's no way that's from being tan."

So I asked my mom, "How come we don't look like each other?"

She sat me down. "I'm going to tell you something, but I don't want you going and telling anyone else. You have different fathers," she began.

"What do you mean?" I asked.

"Their father's name was Ken, like your brother. I left him. He used to beat me. He threw Kenny against the wall one night, so I moved away when I was pregnant with Desiree." She continued. "The last time I saw him, he punched your father and gave him a scar."

"What happened to their father, Ken?" I wondered.

"I don't know and I don't care. I don't ever want to see him again."

"Was my father mean, too?" I had to know.

"No, your father was a nice man. He was just never around. He would disappear for hours, and all he would say is he was riding the subways. That's why I never married him. He never came to see you in the hospital when you were born. He asked me to marry him, but I said, 'No.' And, I left his name off of your birth certificate. Your father's name is Bob Coppola," she revealed.

"Bobacola?" I thought that was a strange name for a man.

"Your dad would come around to see you when you were a baby. He would bring a gallon jug of wine and sit with you on the couch and drink it. I'll never forget when he would leave, you would look out the window and watch him walk down the street with this look on your face, like, 'Who was he?' It used to make me cry. He stopped coming when you were about a year and a half old." Mom stared out the kitchen window as her eyes filled with tears.

"Why?" I asked.

"He got married. I saw him a couple of years ago at a store with some Spanish lady and two little boys." Mom turned the water on to restart the dishes, wiping her face with her sleeve.

"What did he look like?"

"He was Italian. He had brown hair. You have his eyes. He was almost bald, so he always combed his hair over the front. I have a picture of him somewhere." She shut the water off, and I followed her into her bedroom where she found a square photo of a man kissing her. I could only see the side of his head—big ears and a comb-over. He was wearing a green short-sleeved shirt.

"Where is he now?" I questioned.

"I think he's in Queens. His mother used to live in Corona. He never told her about you. She was a strict, religious Catholic and wouldn't have liked your brothers and sister."

Later that evening, I broke the news to my sister Desiree in five-year-old fashion. Jumping up and down on our bed, I chanted,

"Bobacola is my father. Bobacola is my father. Your dad beat Mom and punched my dad. Your dad beat Mom and punched my dad." At least I had a name—and some context. And I think I even had a faint memory of staring out the window watching someone leave.

TROPHY LIFE

The only trophy I ever won was for breaking into a motorcycle shop. My prize: a small, silver cone-shaped cup, with handles flanking each side. It didn't hold milk, as I discovered, due to the curious, purposeful, hole through the base. I displayed it prominently throughout my childhood on a shelf in the bedroom I shared with my two sisters, a story of heroism waiting to be told.

"We used to be bikers," I would begin, with pride, when asked about my trophy. Mom's boyfriend, Richie with no T, was in the Queensboro Motorcycle Club in the early seventies. They were a group of mostly men, who got together in a clubhouse in Queens, New York, to drink, eat, smoke, and plan the next run. They had beards and mustaches, and wore matching leather jackets and vests with the club name on the back. Mom would bring us kids to the club, and my sister Desiree and I would dance all night to Layla and Brown Sugar. The men in the club took my three older brothers under their wing and taught them how to ride. I was too little, but I longed to be special like them.

There were memorable characters in the club. We were told to stay away from Joe Shit the Rag-Man. We didn't know why. He had overgrown body hair, disheveled, torn clothes, and smelled. "Joe blank the Rag-Man has belly button air conditioning," Desiree and I would joke, staring at the hole in his t-shirt right in front of his belly button. There was Whitey, a nice man, named for the dot in his right eyebrow, caused by a birthmark. He owned the New

York Motorcycle shop where Richie worked. He gave all of us kids bicycles one Christmas. The boys got a mini-bike, and Mom got a Harley Davidson 250 dirt bike with an orange gas tank.

"We're going on a run this weekend to Caroga Lake," Mom announced the summer of 1975. She packed up our van with camping gear, the Harley, and us kids, and we followed dozens of bikers on a run to the upstate New York campground.

"There's Ray Honeygranger! There's Camille and Ray August!" we shouted, waving, as the bikers passed our van. It felt cool to belong to the gang, like family.

The campground had a beautiful lake fed by mountain streams. All the bikers congregated at the camp sites, eating, drinking, smoking, and laughing. Mom had fashioned a halter top out of a Harley Davidson t-shirt, and she was beautiful, her long, straight, golden hair framing her soft features.

"It's bath time," Mom said to Desiree and me on the third day. Mom had warmed some stream water on the fire and poured it into the kitchen garbage can she brought from home. "You're first," she said to Desiree, who she picked up and put in the can, cleaning her with Ivory soap. "You're next, Jeneane," Mom declared, and she lowered me in.

"I really have to go to the bathroom," I confessed after a few minutes in the warm water, almost clean.

"Oh shit. Do you have to go too, Desiree?" Mom asked.

"No," she said sheepishly.

"Why not? Did you already go in the water?" Mom demanded to know.

"Yes," Desiree admitted.

"You might as well just go in there too, Jeneane." And so I did, and then rinsed off in the cold stream.

Richie with no T had been living with us for years in our Queens home. He was a tall Italian man with dark hair—the only father I had known, and he was nice to me. Mom and Richie wanted to get married. But, later that summer, Mom sat us kids down for a talk. "Richie's moving to Albuquerque," Mom tearfully explained. "We have to take him to the airport."

"Why?" we asked.

"His mother wants him to go to school there." What Mom didn't say was that Richie's mother wouldn't let him marry her and her five kids.

The day before Richie left, he took my five-year-old hand into his and we went outside for a walk. Richie kneeled down to my eye level. "I'm moving away, but I'll always care about you. I'll come back and visit." Richie explained, giving me a big hug. I thought I was probably his favorite of all of us kids.

"When will you be back?" I asked.

"Not for a while," Richie said, tears forming in his eyes. "You be good for your mother." I felt sad and confused. The last time my Mom and us kids saw Richie, he was boarding a flight to Albuquerque from LaGuardia Airport. We watched as his plane backed away from the gate and took off into the air. I had never seen an object so big.

Mom was heartbroken when Richie left. She started dating Nicky Piscionere, a mechanic at the motorcycle shop, who came to live with us pretty quickly. Then, he moved us to a duplex apartment in Yonkers, New York. One day, when I was home from kindergarten, Mom had an appointment she had to keep, so she dropped me at the motorcycle shop where Nicky worked.

"Are you hungry?" Nicky asked.

"Sure," I responded. Nicky let me have as many doughnuts as I wanted. The shop smelled like the road and car exhaust. It had a concrete floor and motorcycle parts hanging on the walls. Light came in from the glass front door. There was a counter where people picked things up and paid for stuff, and a back room where men worked on the bikes. Intermittent loud vrooms sounded from the repair area as motorcycles were kick-started to see if they worked.

Nicky checked on me every once in a while as I sat in the waiting area. I drew letters and pictures on some paper with a pencil and watched a small TV that was in the corner. A mechanic named Tommy popped in and said, "Hello," winking at me. He seemed younger. I thought he was cute.

I ate everything I was offered—a submarine sandwich, cookies, two slices of pizza, until I couldn't move. It went out the way it came in, as I bent over the toilet, Nicky holding a napkin in front of my frightened face.

"Maybe no more food today," Nicky suggested, cleaning himself up.

"Okay," I agreed.

When it was time to close down the shop, Nicky had me wait out front with Tommy while he turned off all the lights and exited the storefront. Then, he pulled the foldable scissor gate closed and locked the bottom two of the three vertical padlocks.

"Oh fuck!" Nicky yelled, staring through the glass door. "I left the keys on the counter." Nicky tried everything to get back into the shop, including climbing up the scissor gate and attempting to squeeze through the small opening where the gate was unlocked, but he was too big. Then he kneeled down in front of me.

"Jeneane, can you do us a favor? Can you climb up the gate, open the door, and get the keys on the counter? You're the only one who can do this. It would be a big help."

"I'll try." I was scared...the hole in the scissor gate was higher than I had ever climbed. But, I knew it would mean a lot if I could do it.

"Don't worry, we're right here." Nicky offered, trying to comfort me.

I carefully climbed up the front of the gate and swung my left leg through the opening and onto the other side. My body easily fit through the hole as I twisted around and lowered myself down to the ground. I opened the glass door, which wasn't locked, grabbed the keys from the counter and handed them to Nicky. I was met with applause and cheers from Nicky and Tommy.

"Thank you, thank you so much, Jeneane! You saved us! I have something for you," Nicky said. He reopened the shop and went behind the counter to retrieve my prize. "This is for you for saving the day. You're a hero!" Nicky handed me the small silver cup and a 1975 silver dollar. I smiled with pride. I was finally special!

Not long after, Nicky disappeared from our house and was replaced by Tommy the mechanic, who became my younger sister Helene's father. I still have my silver cup and my 1975 silver dollar. They wait in a box in the attic, ready to help me tell the story of when we were bikers, and how I was the hero who saved the day by breaking into the motorcycle shop.

MAN

"Jeneane, Jeneane, come here. I need you." I heard my seven-year-old, older sister Desiree calling from the bathroom of our Yonkers, New York, duplex. I opened the door and peeked in to find her sitting on the toilet. She raised herself slightly off the seat and wiggled her bottom. A respectable doody swung left to right, suspended by a string coming out of her butt. "I'm scared," she said.

"I am, too," I muttered. Even though I was only five, I knew there would be consequences to eating the threads from one of our blankets. Since we were the youngest, we shared a twin bed in the living area of the two-bedroom apartment on Aqueduct Avenue, our makeshift room defined by a long, brown, six-drawer dresser. Our three older brothers were in a room down the hall. And Mom and her boyfriend, Tom, had the other room. Desiree had been pulling threads from the blanket and was delighted by the texture as she balled them up, chewed them a bit, and swallowed them. I tried it once or twice, too.

Our bed was given to us by a family friend and had a white, wooden, horizontal pole as its headboard. In a plot to get tooth fairy money, at night, Desiree and I would repeatedly hit our front teeth on the pole, leaving little pairs of tooth impressions on the length of it. "Think of all the money we could make," I said excitedly. One morning, we woke up completely soaked and wet, as if someone had dumped a bucket of water on us. "What happened?" I asked squirming in the blankets.

"I don't know," Desiree said. We both had to use the toilet in the morning, and everything was so wet that we concluded it couldn't have been one of us. Desiree and I shared a room, and often a bed, for most of our young life. She was there when I tried to suspend a fart in a red Silly Putty egg. I'd pass some air with the egg nearby and quickly close it. Unsure of whether it worked, I'd crack it open and sniff to determine if anything was inside. I couldn't tell, so I tried again.

When we would meet strangers and explain that we were sisters, they would make us stand next to each other. "You don't look anything alike. Is one of you adopted?"

"No," we would respond. "I look like our mom, and she looks like our dad. Plus, she's really tan." The truth was, we had different fathers, but we were definitely full sisters.

At five and seven, we'd stay up at night in the living area, talking and giggling uncontrollably about mostly nothing. Mom's boyfriend, Tom, would come out and yell at us, sometimes spanking us, to go to sleep. One day, we put books in our underwear and made a ruckus to get ourselves in trouble.

"Quiet down, girls," Tom yelled from down the hall. We intentionally raised the volume to antagonize him. "I said be quiet!" Tom appeared, pointing at us with a small blue hairbrush with black bristles. "Turn over," he commanded, ready to hit us with the brush. We gladly obliged and revealed oversized books in our panties. Tom was amused, and thankfully, no one got spanked that day.

As we got older, we became mortal enemies. We would fight day and night. I was jealous of her and wanted to *take her down*. I cried all night when she got the darker pink comb at Easter. Surely they loved her more. She would demand that I clean our room, and I would refuse. Our fist fights would inevitably end with one of us grabbing each other's belly fat and squeezing as hard as we could, leaving dark bruises. Sometimes she'd bite me.

I would plot against her. We finally got bunk beds and I had the top. Using string and toilet paper, I made a garland of small, white ghosts by balling up a sheet of toilet paper, twisting another sheet around it, and linking them together using twine. I looped them length-wise around the top bunk so I could fly them over her in the night, and surely, she would be scared out of her mind. She caught me mid-plan and foiled the scheme.

But I secretly idolized her. I had a crush on all the boys she liked. I had never met Chris Costello, a kid in my sister's class, but I wanted him to be my boyfriend. When I was twelve, her crush, Eugene McCullough, came over to hang out with our brothers. I flirted with him all day, sitting next to him on the couch while she gave me dirty looks from across the room and put her fist in her palm to signal me she was going to get me. And she did after he left. *Whack.* She punched me square in the nose, which bled uncontrollably. My two front teeth hurt for a month.

We became best friends again when I was fifteen and she began visiting us intermittently from the foster home.

"Man, Man, I need you," I screamed from the toilet. Desiree appeared in the doorway. Man became my nickname for her from that day forward.

"What's the matter?"

"I think I got my period, Man. Look." I showed her the evidence.

"Yay, Jeneane! You're a woman now. Honestly, I thought you were gonna be sterile." She handed me a box of O.B. tampons. "These are Mom's big ones. You know how to use them? Let me know if you need help."

"Yeah, I know what to do." I had already read the paper insert countless times, and I navigated the event easily. It brought me back to the day, ten years ago, when I helped Desiree on the toilet with her string doody.

"How do I get it out of me? What if it's attached?" Desiree asked in desperation.

"Take a piece of toilet paper and pull it out with your fingers," I said. She did what I suggested, it came out, and she was back to normal. Plus, I knew exactly what to do when it happened to me the next day and no one was around. Clearly, that's what full sisters are for.

JAIL TURD

"**Y**ou know they strip search you before you go in," my brother Edward revealed. "Nene ran out into the hallway naked, and we had to chase her down. Everyone saw." Nene was my five-year-old sister Helene's nickname. She would later immortalize it with an ankle tattoo.

"No way. You have to take your clothes off? Is it private?"

"Nope, everyone's in the same room. Even other visitors."

"Oh no." I was seriously regretting my decision to visit my brother Derek in jail. What if people saw my eleven-year-old, flabby, white, prepubescent body? No one had seen me naked since the seventies—except my oldest brother Kenny.

One day in sixth grade, I really thought I was doing my classmate, Cathy, a favor when I picked a lone head louse out of the part in her hair, killed it with my fingernail, and showed it to her.

"You better tell your mom," I said with authority.

I knew about lice because I just had it. There was an epidemic during that school year in Saugerties, New York, and I had long, thick red hair—a perfect place to nest.

Mom had gotten a prescription for Kwell shampoo, and she made us five kids use it. Then she tried getting rid of the eggs from our hair with a nit comb, as directed. "You're infested," Mom said looking through my hair under a bright light. "I'm going to have to cut these eggs out." Mom snipped any hair she saw with white nits close to the root, removing random chunks with her special barber scissors. "This will thin your hair out." But, it didn't work. A couple of weeks later, I could feel itchy crawling on my scalp. I tried to catch the bastards between my fingertips, but it was like trying to pinch a minnow. I knew I needed to treat myself again with the leftover Kwell.

Our rented house in West Saugerties had two bathrooms. The main floor had a tub-shower combo near all the kids' bedrooms. One evening, when my mom was working at the restaurant, and my brothers and sisters seemed preoccupied, I grabbed the Kwell and headed into the bathroom for my treatment.

First, I read the directions. "Avoid contact with eyes. If contact occurs, rinse with cool tap water." This scared me. I did not want this bug stuff in my eyes. I knew my brother Edward had a pair of swimming goggles, so I slipped out of the bathroom and snuck into his room. I could hear that there were some neighborhood kids in my brother Kenny's room next door. I grabbed the goggles from the bottom drawer of Edward's dresser and returned to the bathroom to complete my mission.

The goggles weren't the streamlined Speedos of today. They looked like Minion goggles with thick, yellow rims and a black strap. I undressed, goggled up, and bent over the side of the tub to turn on the faucet—my chunked-out, crazy hair poking in every direction. Suddenly, the bathroom door swung open. I stood up, looked over, and made eye-to-goggle contact with my brother Kenny for a split second. He quickly escaped, slamming the door behind him.

A loud cackle came from the hallway. "I just saw some ugly naked fat thing with yellow goggles on," I heard him tell his friends, laughing uncontrollably. I was embarrassed, but the image of Kenny being confronted by an "ugly naked fat thing with yellow goggles on" was so funny, I giggled to myself, locked the door, and continued delousing.

Would the strip search at Derek's jail be just as humiliating? I wondered if there were a way I could get out of it, but I hadn't seen Derek since right after he was arrested.

About a year earlier, when we were still living in Yonkers, New York, I came home from staying the night at my best friend Maureen's apartment next door. Mom was strangely home. "Hi, Mom. Are you off from work today?"

"Didn't anybody tell you?" my mom said in a tone that clearly indicated something was wrong.

"What do you mean? What happened?"

"Derek was arrested last night for armed robbery. He and another kid robbed a gas station with a bee bee gun."

"What? Oh my god. Where is he? Is he okay?" I started crying. Derek was only fifteen, but he looked like a man, about six-foot-two at the time, brown skin and hair, being of mixed race.

"He's in the Yonkers jail. I'm going down there later to see him. You can come if you want to."

Derek's bizarre request from the night before started to make sense. "Hey, Jeneane-I, do you have any makeup I could borrow?" Derek asked in an unusually friendly tone. He called me Jeneane-I because someone once spelled my name J-A-N-I-N-E, and I thought that was how it was pronounced.

"Sure," I replied. I was excited to help my brother with his request. He was usually horribly mean and threatening to me and my older sister Desiree.

"I *will* kill you if you tell Mom you did the dishes," he had promised me once, grabbing my throat and pushing me against the kitchen wall. Mom left a chore list on the fridge, and doing the dishes paid four dollars. He wanted to do them for the money, but after three days, they sat, and I couldn't take it anymore. Mom found out I did the dishes, and Derek came home to make good on his threat. Thankfully, Mom's transient boyfriend, Jamie, stood guard and helped save me from being murdered that day.

31

"The only makeup I have is this Barbie makeup." I gave Derek the makeup that came with a giant Barbie head someone had given me as a gift. You could style her hair with a plastic curling iron, and apply creamy blue eye shadow, blush, lip gloss, and mascara. "Are you going to scare your friends?" I asked.

"Thanks, Jeneane-I. Yeah, I'm going to scare my friends," Derek snickered. He took the blue eye shadow, which came in a lipstick-like twist-up tube, and colored in his forehead and around his hairline and face. Then, he looked in the bathroom mirror, thought about it, and washed it off, leaving some blue residue around the perimeter of his hairline. I headed off to my friend Maureen's house for a sleepover. The next time I saw him, he was crying behind a reinforced glass door at the local jail.

I stood there with my mother and my little sister Helene, looking at him through the glass. I could see the blue makeup near his sideburns. "You are so stupid," I told him. I knew he couldn't hurt me from behind that door, and I was so mad at him for what he did to our family. But, I did love him.

The next year, I was preparing for the strip search that would happen at the juvenile jail called Chodikee in Highland, New York, where he was transferred. All of my brothers and sisters, my mom, and her boyfriend, Lenny, were going to visit him that day.

"I'm going to bring him this," my older sister Desiree shared, holding up a pink, heart-shaped pillow with a white ruffle trim. She made it in home economics class.

"I'm going to bring him this." I held out the clay sculpture I made in art class. It was a small, brown basinet with a round baby head resting at the top. A clay blanket covered the baby's body. I painted the blanket red on top and white where it folded over.

"There's no strip search," my mother told me on the side before we got into the car. *Oh, thank goodness*, I thought. All seven of us piled into the Dodge Charger and drove an hour from West Saugerties to Highland. We pulled up to the facility—a gray stone, municipal looking building with square windows and green landscaping. We walked into the visitors' area, and several male guards took down our names and wanded us with a metal detector.

"What's this for?" a guard asked, examining my sculpture closely. Boop, boop, went the metal detector.

"I'm giving it to my brother." He rolled his eyes, wanded it, and gave it back. Then, one of the guards walked us into a windowless room with yellow, cinderblock walls, cafeteria-like tables and chairs, and a bathroom. We sat and waited for Derek.

When Derek walked in, he seemed very different. He was taller, and his gestures were weird. He punctuated every sentence with, "You know what I'm sayin'?" and pointed to himself with all ten fingers when he spoke, like Howie Mandel in his comedy show from the early eighties. He hugged Mom hard for at least a minute, tears streaming down both of their faces. He hugged the rest of us one at a time before we all sat down at one of the tables. I couldn't wait to give him my gift.

"What's going on with you, Jeneane-I," Derek asked about thirty minutes into the visit. I was glad he wasn't going to take revenge on me for calling him stupid at the Yonkers jail.

"I brought you this." I handed him the sculpture. He studied it.

"What is this Jeneane-I?" Derek asked. "A turd in a bathtub?" He was right. To the average juvenile prisoner, the brown baby head in the basinet, with the blanket, looked like a round doody ball with a face, floating in a tub.

"It's a baby in a crib." I muttered. "I made it in art class."

"I can't do anything with this. I can't keep this. The guys in this place will kick my ass. You gotta take this turd in a bathtub home. You know what I'm sayin'?" He pushed it toward me. I pulled it close and wondered whether Derek would like the heart-shaped ruffled pillow my older sister Desiree brought for him.

"I can't keep this either," he said examining the pillow. "This is girly shit. You can't have girly shit in a place like this. You know what I'm sayin'?" Again, he was right.

We finished the visit and said our goodbyes, not knowing when Derek would be able to come home. I took my turd in a bathtub home with me that day and put it on my windowsill to wait for his return.

WEARING THE
FAMILY PANTS

Growing up in the seventies and eighties, the biggest challenge for most kids I knew was how to get their parents to buy them stuff advertised during Saturday morning cartoons: Matchbox cars, Twister, Lite Brite, Big Wheels, and Stretch Armstrong. Mine was pants. Being pants insecure was my life. At any given time, I had zero to two pairs of pants I could wear in public. It was partly because Mom couldn't afford to buy me and my five siblings clothes, and partly because I was constantly growing and misshapen.

One day in seventh grade, an unfamiliar pair of pants appeared folded on my bed. I was curious and excited. I picked them up and shook them out. They were dark blue, straight leg, corduroys. They didn't look like they belonged to any of my siblings, so naturally, I tried them on. They fit my twelve-year old body better than any other pants I owned—not too big or too small, slim in the hips, and long enough so they weren't floods. I figured my mom had picked them up at a second hand store and thought I might like them.

The next school day, I was eager to wear them with my red, short-sleeved top, accented with three large white buttons down the front. I walked the hallways at Saugerties Junior High with confidence, finally without pants embarrassment. A whoop-whoop sound accompanied me as my thighs rubbed the corduroy fabric together with every step.

What will I do tomorrow? I thought. *No one will notice if I wear them again,* I concluded.

My first pants memory was of melon-colored polyester slacks with an elastic waistband, a pleat down the front, and a permanent, folded-up cuff. It was the mid-seventies and Mom had gotten them second-hand. I put them on one morning before kindergarten at P.S. 11 in Yonkers, New York, and did the things a five-year-old does before school—climb on the furniture, run down the hallway, play with the temporary dog, Socks. The cuffs slowly came undone until I was walking on the fabric that fell below my sneakers. "Mom, my pants are ripped," I said before we walked out the door for school. She took a close look at them.

"Hold on," she insisted. Mom grabbed the stapler from the shelf in the living room and stapled the cuffs up so I could make it through the school day in my melon slacks.

"What were you thinking about for Christmas?" Mom asked us kids a few months later.

"Racecars," my older brothers said.

"A doll," my older sister said.

"Pants," I said to my mother. That evening, Mom and her latest boyfriend, Nicky, sat me down for an important talk. "Santa can't afford pants this year, but he can afford material so I can make you pants. Is that ok?" Mom asked.

"I guess so," I replied. I wasn't really sure what that meant. When could I wear the pants? What would they look like?

On Christmas morning, I unwrapped a stack of black corduroy fabric, some orange embroidery thread, and a pattern that my mom told me said "Simplicity" across the top. I set it aside on the coffee table, knowing my mother would need to get the sewing machine out and work on it. While my older brothers and sister played with their new toys, I sat alone, tears welling up in my eyes. What did I do? Should I have asked for a toy too? Posing for the Christmas picture in front of the tree, I appeared to be holding a handful of trash covered with tinsel as my gift.

A week later, Mom got to work on my new pants. She sewed two pairs of black corduroys with an elastic waistband, and a square-headed orange robot embroidered on the back pockets. "Come here and try these on," she said.

I put them on and they fit! I committed to wearing my new pants on alternating kindergarten days, but eventually the identical pants confused me and I couldn't tell them apart.

My pants confusion continued. At age ten, Mom took my older sister Desiree and me to the Gap. She bought us each the same two pairs of pants in identical sizes: a pair of jeans and a pair of forest green corduroys.

"I think these are baggy," I observed looking in the dressing room mirror. They were two sizes too big.

"They'll shrink, and then you'll grow into them," Mom said. After about a week, my sister and I couldn't tell whose pants we were wearing.

About a year later, I got treated to surprise bonus pants. Mom was dating a petite but muscular and mustached Croatian waiter from Trevi's, the restaurant where she bartended. We called him Lenny, and he lived with us in our three-bedroom apartment in Yonkers, New York, near Yonkers Raceway.

"Would you like to go to the flea market?" Lenny asked my sisters and me one spring Sunday morning on his day off.

"Sure," we said. On foot, we crossed Yonkers Avenue as a group, and Lenny paid the two dollar admission to get us into the flea market at the raceway. People were selling pants!

"You want to try on some pants?" Lenny asked.

"Sure," I said and grabbed two pairs of Corniche brand jeans and went into the dressing room.

"You can get two pairs," Lenny said. I scored one white and one purple pair of designer jeans that day, plus a pair of stylish Mary Jane slipper shoes. Mom might have cautioned me about the pants colors if she had been there. The next day, I stained the white ones picking up a folding chair that had rusty water in it. The purple pair ripped when they got caught on the metal thing poking out of the sofa. I covered the tear with a heart-shaped, denim iron-on patch I found in the sewing box.

The patched purple pair lasted almost through the sixth grade, where I was known as "The Girl with the Purple Pants," when we moved back to upstate New York. By the time the blue corduroy jeans appeared on my bed in seventh grade, I was virtually pants-less.

I felt good in the blue corduroys, and I wore them every day to school, until the friction thwarted me. Thirty days of my legs rubbing the ribs of the fabric together—whoop, whoop, whoop—burned two adjacent holes into the crotch of my pants, until my thighs chafed from repeated skin-to-skin contact. I tried sewing the area with some black thread, and put some Vaseline on the rash, but within a day, the rubbing undid my work. One afternoon, my Health class gathered, legs crossed, on the gymnasium floor for an anti-drug assembly. A friendly classmate approached me. "Do you know you have holes in your pants? Down there."

"Yeah, I know. I need new pants." The pants insecurity returned full force.

❋ ❋ ❋

"Those are my pants," my oldest brother Kenny said when I got home from school that day. "I've been looking all over for those. You've been wearing my pants?"

"Really? Oh sorry. I thought they were mine. You can have them back. They have holes in them."

"No thanks," Kenny said taking one look. "You can keep them."

Thankfully, I haven't burned out a crotch in years. And now, I regularly donate my gently used pants in the hopes that they will appear, folded up on someone's bed, ready to provide some pants security.

HIGH HOPES

Small flecks of free weed appeared in my change purse well into my teens. How it got there was a simple story. In the early eighties, it seemed that everyone cool in Saugerties, New York, smoked weed, including my older brothers. So when the kid at the back of the junior-senior high school bus asked me and my friend Jennifer Gurvich if we wanted some, we said yes.

"Do you have anything to put it in?" the kid asked.

I took out a small, brown change purse with a brass clasp, dumped out the coins and barrettes, and held it open. "I have this," I offered. With his thumb and forefinger, the kid transferred three to four pinches of loose weed into my change purse. I clasped it shut.

"You can pay me whenever," the kid said, concluding my first and only drug deal. Jennifer and I couldn't wait to get home later and try it out. Even though I was twelve, it wasn't my first encounter with weed. I had first smoked pot three days before my last birthday.

What's this? I thought, finding a prescription drug bottle with green stuff in my mother's underwear drawer. I skimmed some weed from her stash and put it in tin foil until I could figure out what to do with it. My friend Maureen would be visiting from our old Yonkers neighborhood the next week for my birthday, and I thought we could use it.

"I stole some of Mom's pot. Let's smoke it when Maureen gets here," I revealed to my older sister Desiree. "I have an idea for rolling papers to make joints."

My mother had an old English literature book from a college course she had taken. On the cover was a stern-looking pale queen with a paper fan around her neck—perfect bathroom reading material. The pages were tissue paper-like, very close to the consistency of rolling papers. *The blank pages are perfect for joints,* I thought.

One day, when I was home alone, I cut two blank pages out of the book and shaped those pages into rectangles the size of rolling papers. I carefully folded the paper and sprinkled in the weed, making three joints with a process I had learned from the Cheech & Chong movies. I secured the joints with Scotch tape, and stowed them until Maureen's visit.

"Let's wait until dark and smoke these at the Big Three," I said to my sister Desiree and Maureen the first Friday of her visit. It was July. The Big Three was a natural watering hole about a mile from where we lived in West Saugerties. It had a cool mountain stream and a twenty foot waterfall that plunged into a clear pool. Maureen had been my best friend since the third grade. We lived directly next door to each other in Yonkers and hated each other at first. Then, after bonding over learning how to ride a bike, we became inseparable. When my family moved to Saugerties, Maureen's mother promised she'd be able to visit often.

At about eight-thirty p.m., I grabbed the joints, and some matches, and we headed up the road to the Big Three. As we walked, it got very dark. "Oh my gosh. I can't see anything," I said.

"Neither can I," Maureen and Desiree added. "Let's hold hands." Hand-in-hand, we turned down the unpaved road toward the Big Three, randomly tripping over rocks and debris. Eyes appeared and disappeared in the woods surrounding us.

"Maybe we should just smoke it here," Desiree suggested. We could hear the waterfall, but it was too dark to see anything, and we were spooked.

"Okay, I'm fine with that." We sat down under a tree, and I pulled out a joint, lit it, and took the first toke, trying to hold it in like Cheech & Chong. The smoke from the weed combined with the burning college book paper and Scotch tape choked me into a coughing fit. "Here," I offered the joint to Maureen.

Maureen and Desiree took hits from the joint and began coughing. We all sounded as if we had been tear-gassed. We finished one joint and headed home in the dark, holding hands. "Do you feel anything?" I asked.

"Not really," they said. Neither did I.

Now, I was going to get a chance to smoke pot again with my new friend Jennifer. Jennifer lived with her mom in a small, cabin-like house about a hundred yards across a field from me. So, one day when her mom wasn't home, I headed over with my brown change purse.

"I have some pants that might fit you, if you want them," Jennifer said. She went to her room and retrieved several pairs of pants. The beige corduroy and brown Sweet-Orr brand pants fit me pretty well, so I put them aside to take home. I was grateful for the additional pants, even though few people were still wearing Sweet-Orrs.

"Do you know vanilla has thirty-five percent alcohol in it? You can get drunk off of it," I explained. Jennifer opened her spice cabinet and found a tiny bottle of imitation vanilla extract. We both took a sip.

"That's disgusting," we agreed.

I continued. "Nutmeg gets you high, too. I learned in Health class that they use it to get high in jail."

"Really? Let's try it." Jennifer was game. The nutmeg tasted terrible, too.

"You know what else gets you high?" I asked, "morning glory

seeds. I have a few at home I saved from a plant." Stuff that gets you high seemed to be what we had in common, even though I don't think I had ever really been high before. "Do you have any rolling papers?" I asked.

"We don't need them," Jennifer said and opened the refrigerator. Then, came a teaching moment I would never forget. Jennifer found a large carrot in her fridge and pulled a potato peeler from a drawer. She cut off the big end of the carrot and dug out a hole, long-ways through the center, just short of poking out the other end. She then carved another hole through the top near the in-tact end to form a complete connection with the center core hole. She took a small piece of tin foil, pushed it into the top hole, and poked tiny openings in it with the tip of a pen. She then inhaled through the open end. "See, it's a homemade pipe." I thought that was very cool.

Jennifer put some of the change purse weed into the foil, lit it, and inhaled through the carrot pipe. Then, I took a couple of hits. We coughed a lot, and then Jennifer ate the carrot.

"Do you feel anything?" I asked.

"No, not really," Jennifer said.

"Neither do I." I gave the rest of the pot to Jennifer, but I always had tiny pieces of weed in the bottom of that change purse. And, we never paid that kid.

ESCAPE FROM NEW YORK

When Mom and Ritchie with a T sat us down over Christmas break and told us we were moving to Wyoming, I thought it was somewhere near China. "Where's that," I asked? My brothers, Kenny and Edward, and sisters, Desiree and Helene, wondered too. I had heard the word before, but I didn't know what it was.

"It's about 1800 miles away, in the Midwest." Mom replied. "Ritchie was born in Laramie, and thinks we could get good jobs in the oil industry. Plus Anna's brother lives in Casper." Anna was a new friend my mother had met through Ritchie when they started dating a few months earlier. Anna had two daughters who were buddies with my sister Desiree and me.

Mom started dating Ritchie when Lenny, the Croatian waiter, was still living with us. I remember Ritchie came to the door one afternoon and French-kissed my mother while Lenny was in the living room. After a big fight, and Lenny driving the Dodge Charger into a mud-hole in the woods, we never saw him or his car again. Then, Ritchie moved in.

Ritchie was tall, with a slim build and dark brown head and facial hair. He wore "Cat Diesel" hats and worked construction. He liked to laugh and gave us alcohol to see what would happen. On my brother Kenny's eighteenth birthday, just after I turned twelve, Ritchie, my brother Edward, and I were sitting at the picnic table in the front yard. "You wanna try this?" Ritchie offered, pushing a shot of Black Velvet whisky my way. "You gotta drink it all at once."

"Ok," I said, picked up the shot glass, and drank it in one gulp. A severe fire burned through my chest. It was a pain I had never felt before. "Oh my god," I gasped, breathing deeply and running into the house for some water, while Ritchie laughed. I never did another shot until tequila when I was twenty-one.

My brother Edward drank too much Black Velvet and ended up lying on a mop head in the backyard, pleading for canned corn. "Corn, corn," he begged, which my sister Desiree handed to him in the can with a spoon. Four months later, we were talking about moving again.

"Casper, like the ghost?" Edward quipped.

"Yeah, kinda." My mom giggled. "We can't afford to live here anymore. I can't find work. We're leaving after New Year's, so you're not going back to school. You can only take the bare essentials. Ritchie said the people there are nice, down-home folks, and we'd love it."

I was glad I didn't have to go back to school, so Wyoming sounded like a good idea. Mr. Barth, my seventh grade Health teacher, was waiting for me to complete an "Overview," which meant I had to get a book from the library, read it, and summarize it—a task I was trying to avoid. But, I was also nervous to move. We had been living in a four-bedroom, two-bath, house in West Saugerties, New York, for almost two years. There was plenty of space for us kids, and room to play outside. We had friends. There was a large field to the side of the house where we could play tag and Crack-About in the summer, and a natural swimming hole up the road. In the winter, there were nearby sleigh-riding hills, ice skating ponds, and a yard to make snowmen. I would sit on the concrete slab covering the well on the side of the house and pull bark off of cedar to make walking sticks.

We had moved five times in New York since I was born in Queens —to Yonkers, to Lake Katrine, to Kingston, to Yonkers again, and then to West Saugerties—and this was my favorite house—woods for exploring and building makeshift tree forts, wild blackberry bushes and pear trees, and the buzz of late summer cicadas. But, the landlord was raising the rent. At our last apartment in Yonkers, Mom tended bar in New Rochelle at night, and brought home good tips, which she'd unload from her bra in a wadded up ball. I straightened three hundred and twelve dollar bills from her boobies one day. The move to upstate was, in part, because my brother Derek committed a crime while my mom was work-ing nights and was in jail. But money got tight. Ritchie and my brother Kenny had been working for a fencing company, and jobs were scarce in the winter.

"What do you mean by the bare essentials?" Desiree asked.

"You can only take what you can't live without." Mom explained.

"What about the furniture and Pepper?" Edward inquired. Pepper was our black and tan, Shepherd-Lab mix.

"We're going to have to sell the furniture." Mom said. "And Pepper can come. Anything we take has to fit on the back of Ritchie's pick-up truck or in the trunk of the car."

After Lenny left with his Dodge Charger, Mom bought a four-door, gold, 1973 Chrysler New Yorker. The plan was, we'd all ride in the car on the way to Wyoming and tow the truck, packed with our belongings, Beverly Hillbillies style. Pepper could ride in the cab of the truck.

"Are you coming, Kenny?" I asked because he was eighteen and could do what he wanted.

"I don't know," he replied.

Now, we had to figure out our bare essentials. It was almost too easy for me. I didn't have any toys or working bicycles. My older brothers had used my pink Huffy Sweet Thunder 2 bike until the fragile female-rated frame and pedals broke. I opted to get rid of all of the clothes that didn't fit me, which left me with only a few outfits. Mom had a second-hand store come look at our furniture. They offered us one hundred seventy-five dollars for it, and they wouldn't take it all. Ritchie took the rest to the dump.

On January 3, 1983, two adults, five kids, and a dog started on the journey from West Saugerties, New York to Casper, Wyoming, with only two hundred seventy-five dollars and no plan for when we got there. Mom and Ritchie strategized the trip so they could drive straight for thirty-six hours and pay no tolls through Pennsylvania, Ohio, Indiana, Illinois, Iowa, Nebraska, and finally, Wyoming. Mom packed peanut butter and jelly and tuna fish sandwiches, and we made oatmeal at rest stops using our electric coffee percolator. I slept on the right door in the back seat with the pillow I had made by sewing up the holes of an old t-shirt. Us kids farted a lot and blamed each other. We raced to claim the nicer cars that drove by. "My car," we'd shout when a Trans Am passed. Somewhere in Iowa, a cop stopped us and told Ritchie he couldn't sleep in the cab of the pickup truck in tow. It got colder and colder as we drove.

We arrived in Casper at about four a.m. on the morning of January 5. It was dark and bitter cold. "C'mon kids, we're here. They said Pepper could stay." I awoke to see we were in the parking lot of the Red and White Motel. It was a one story building, shaped like an upside-down, squared-off U, with cars parked in front of the doors, and plowed snow piled near the edges. "Let's leave the stuff in the truck till tomorrow. We're in room five." Emerging from the car, I stretched my legs and grabbed my garbage bag of spare clothes and toiletries from the trunk. The air smelled sweet and crisp.

"Ritchie and I are gonna take the bedroom with Helene, and you four can stay on the pull-out." Room number five opened into a small living room with a bathroom to the left, a tiny kitchen in the back, and a bedroom to the right. A clock radio rested on the end table next to the sofa bed, and a nineteen-inch TV sat opposite. Who knew that in two weeks, we'd be watching ourselves on that very TV in a story on the local news.

HOMEMADE UNDERWEAR

Why would a thirteen-year-old construct a pair of underwear out of a fuchsia velour sweater and wear them to gym class? Looking back, there were at least three reasons: I was bored, I liked soft stuff, and I had an unacceptable level of viable underpants.

Let me explain.

It was fall of 1984. About a year and a half earlier, Mom had decided to sell everything from our rented house in upstate New York and move five kids, a dog, and her boyfriend to Wyoming in search of jobs in the oil industry. Now, with only an older brother and younger sister left under the same roof, someone was stretching out my underwear.

I simply did not know what was happening. I thought maybe Mom started wearing them to her job at the gas station, pumping gas and stretching out my underwear, day after day, but there wasn't enough time for her to have stretched out all eight pairs until they were that big, that fast. And I knew I wasn't losing weight. That was somewhat unlikely on a diet of rolled hamburger meat and free government cheese.

Stretched-out underwear is a junior high hazard, especially when you're a new kid in 1980s gym shorts. With each jog, they would fall. Supported only by the crotch of my shorts, they would inevitably drape loosely down the sides of each outer thigh like an unmarked, misshapen Survivor buff.

"I can see your underwear."

"I know," I would say pulling them back up and running with one hand pressed against my waist. I thought about using safety pins, but the only inconspicuous remedy was to tie a tiny knot in one side—an unreliable, mini ball that would poke my hip all day long. This was a problem, and I intended to solve it.

We had moved to the prairie outside of Casper, Wyoming. Mom had managed to get two acres of property with a three-bedroom mobile home, but the catch was, there was no running water. We'd have to use an outhouse until she could save up enough money to drill a well and put in septic.

The outhouse was a four-by-four wooden shack with a slanted metal roof. Inside, a solid bench was built across the back of the structure with a single hole and a toilet seat in the center. There was an extension cord coming from the trailer to power a free-standing flood light that hung on a nail hook.

It was a self-contained outhouse...there was no hole in the ground because Mom didn't want to contaminate the land and the future well. Everything dropped into a fifty-five gallon drum that was cut in half like the can in the Ginsu commercial. There was a side door where you could exchange an empty half-drum for a full half-drum. That job usually fell to my brother Edward and me. We'd glove up, grab each side of the drum, promise not to rock it too much, and carry it about twenty feet from the outhouse. Then, we'd pour in diesel fuel and light it on fire. It would burn for a couple of hours, creating an indescribably vile cloud of smoke. After it cooled, we'd lift it onto the back of the pick-up, drive it seventy-five feet to the other side of the property, and dump it into an empty hole in the ground that was prematurely dug for a septic tank.

The outhouse had its seasonal charm. In the summertime, you could enjoy the smell of diesel fuel mixed with excrement, coupled with flies that would periodically land on your buttocks and crawl around while you were minding your own business.

The winter was a much more memorable experience. Extreme cold makes everything freeze. Five people pooping in the same spot of a halved fifty-five gallon drum causes a gradual build up of waste product, like a fouled stalagmite. Eventually, the stalagmite of ice poop would be tall enough to touch your bottom when you sat down, so you had to prepare. We kept a length of two-by-four in the outhouse so we could beat down the tower of frozen poop before settling in.

In the glory days of the outhouse, there were a couple of exciting additions to its charm. First, Mom gladly accepted an elk hide from a passing hunter who didn't want it. She planned to "tan" it. The first step in tanning was throwing the elk hide on top of the outhouse to dry it out. It covered the entire roof and draped down the sides, a fact not lost on the neighborhood dogs who tried several times to run off with it.

Second, Mom bought twenty-five baby chicks for twenty-five cents each from a hatchery in the dead of winter. With nowhere else to put them, they ended up in a small box in the outhouse with only the flood light to keep them warm. The chicks had a tendency to trample each other to death as they gathered around the flood light, which was their sole source of heat.

So, at this perfect moment, when you felt the urge to go, you'd put on the family winter coat and moon boots placed conveniently by the front door of the trailer, head outside to enter the outhouse with the elk hide toupee, grab the doomed two-by-four to beat down the pile of frozen poop, and then sit on a cold toilet seat to do your business in front of the chirping, homicidal baby chicks who kept igniting their feathers on the scorching hot flood light.

So, in my spare time, I decided to make my own pair of underwear.

The good news is I had already made a small hand-sewn purse out of a pair of light pink corduroys using the fly as the zipper, so I had some experience in the area.

First, I gathered my resources. I had an old, spent pair of underwear to use as a pattern. Mom had some quarter-inch white elastic in her sewing box that she let me use, which was probably left over from her hippie days when she made her own clothes. I had several pants and shirts that had become too small for me, including the soft, hand-me-down, fuchsia velour sweater, which I had trouble parting with. Naturally, I selected it for my project. I clearly didn't care how the thick fabric would look under my clothes. On the hierarchy of underwear needs, you have to have working panties before you could worry about panty lines.

I started by using a seam ripper to make a pattern from the existing underwear, and then I carefully traced and cut the pieces from the sweater, including an extra crotch piece for interior velour. Using purple thread, I began assembling the pieces by hand until I had a discernible, high-waisted bikini brief in fuchsia velour with no elastic. After several trial runs, I added the elastic by creating a circle, sized for the waist band, and stretching it between my knees while hand sewing it to the garment. When I finished the waist, I made the executive decision to forego the elastic around the legs. I figured I didn't need it. Plus, I planned to use my time to make a matching shoulder bag out of the same fuchsia velour fabric.

On the next gym day, I put on my new cozy pair of underwear, got dressed, grabbed my matching purse, and headed off to eighth grade. On the way to the bus stop, I realized the elastic decision was a poor one. Mom had given me a butt that looked like the back of a 1990 Honda CRX, and I had nothing to keep eight inches of fuchsia velour fabric from bunching up into the crack of my behind. I tried to pull it out when no one was looking, but it quickly went back to its natural position, like a startled opossum.

Carefully changing for gym class, I heard, "Those are cool underwear," from behind. "Thank you," I said turning back around to my locker to quickly to end the conversation. How did she see them under my shirt? Usually when classmates said they liked my clothes or sneakers, what they were really trying to say is, "I and my friends have been discussing your general appearance, and we disapprove. We thought we'd try to get your thoughts so we could customize our plan to humiliate you."

"I like your purse, too. It's cool that they match. Where did you get those?"

"I made them from an old shirt."

"Really? That's pretty cool."

"Thanks."

I finished changing and headed out to gym. This time, each jog concentrated the fabric between my buttocks until I experienced the kind of chafing known only to the young and old. No one noticed, though, so I just pretended to be normal.

At home, I removed the underwear and put them in the dirty clothes with a plan to apply the elastic to the legs before trying them again. Meanwhile, I put on a knotted pair. That weekend at the laundromat, Mom asked who gave me the fancy underpants, so I filled her in.

"Mom, do you know how my underwear got stretched out? Have you been wearing them?"

"I don't think so. Mine are stretched out, too. Who is doing that to us?"

"I don't know. Who would do that?"

"It's the industrial dryers," explained the woman behind us. "It eats up elastic and lace and stuff like that."

I never did get around to putting the elastic into the legs of the fuchsia velour underwear. And, we never did get that well and septic. Instead, I moved back to New York and went to college so I could afford to buy as much underwear as I wanted and wash them in my own laundry room.

And I never wear thongs. Ever.

ROCK STAR

I should have known better than to take medical advice from my mother, although she did go to nursing school for three months in the early sixties. Once, I told her it hurt when I swallowed, and her advice was clear and impossible: Don't swallow.

The problem was, I had something growing at the bottom of my chin, right in the middle. It wasn't any kind of mole or pimple that I had seen before. It was like a tiny, skin-colored, deflated balloon, and it didn't hurt when I squeezed or pulled at it. Being new at my junior high—a recent transplant to Casper, Wyoming from upstate New York—I was trying hard not to draw attention to myself.

"What's that on your chin? It looks weird." Tori Updike asked in the lunch line.

"I don't know...I'm gonna ask my mom to go to the doctor." I didn't realize until that moment that other people noticed it. I had to do something. But for now, I wanted my lunch, and I loved institutional food. It was free, prepared by others, and there were always a variety of things to eat. With turkey cubes and gravy, you got mashed potatoes, green beans, fruit cup, and milk.

"Free," I said to the lunch lady at the cash register, and showed her my meal ticket with the letter A in the corner. B was reduced, and C was full price, so everyone knew we were poor. I grabbed the empty end of a table and sat by myself to enjoy my first meal of the day.

"It's a wart from where you had your stitches," Mom said. "You don't need to go to the doctor. But I wouldn't cut it off or you'll hemorrhage. I'll get you some Compound W." Mom was getting ready for her evening shift at Highway Oil, the only full-service gas station in Casper. The air in the trailer's single bathroom was filled with cigarette smoke, Adorn hairspray, and coffee. She had on a white work shirt with a patch above the left-hand breast pocket that said, "Helene." Her blonde hair was fresh from hot rollers as she applied thick, blue eye shadow. "That'll take care of it," she said.

She was probably right. When I was three, we still lived in Queens, New York. Mom had company over and us kids were told to stay out of the living room. I tried going to sleep, but I had to pee really bad, and there were no grownups to help. There was no way I was going to ask my older brothers or sister because they would call me a baby. In a panic, I went into the pitch black bathroom and tried to find the light switch, but it was a pull string that was too high for me to reach. I climbed onto the toilet seat, but I still couldn't reach. So, I climbed onto the tank, and BAM! I fell chin-first onto the toilet tank lid. My chin split open, I screamed, and Mom called the police to take us to the emergency room. After more screaming, and a thousand needles poking my chin, as I lay swaddled and restrained in my Harley Davidson t-shirt and underwear, I went home with a small, black beard of three stitches holding together my toilet tank cut. Ten years later, I had a wart.

"Here's your Compound W," Mom said the next day, tossing the bottle my way. I remembered using it on feet warts when I was about seven. Finally, I could get rid of this thing.

"Apply, let it dry, repeat once or twice a day up to 12 weeks," the label said. So, I opened the little bottle, applied it with the glass applicator, and waited for the wart to peel off like my feet ones did in the seventies. After one day, nothing happened, so I applied it again. Then, each day again, and again, and again. But all that happened was layer after layer of dried Compound W built up on the wart until it was a hard, gray ball that moved at the base. I took a pair of scissors and tried to cut off the dried Compound W from the tip, but it was too firm.

I saw my mother a few days later as she was getting ready for work, applying mascara and blush. "Mom, the Compound W isn't helping. It's just building up on there, and nothing's happening."

"Let me take a look," she said and pulled my face close to hers. "Take a piece of string and tie it around it. It'll fall off by itself."

This sounded like a logical plan. I had heard of people tying rope around a bull's testicles, which would eventually fall off. Desperate, I found the sewing box on the bottom shelf of a built-in bookcase by the front door of the trailer. There were a few colors to choose from, and without a second thought, I chose the black thread and took it to the bathroom. I looped a length of thread around the base of my wart, tied a knot as tight as I could, and snipped the ends. It looked and felt like a small pebble sewn to bottom-center of my chin with a single black stitch. And the next day, I went to school.

"What is that thing on your chin?" Vickie Lipps asked in my second period English class.

"Well, I had this wart or something growing from my chin, and I tried putting Compound W on it, but that just built up, so my mother told me to tie a string around it and it would fall off," I said in one breath with a straight face.

"It looks so weird. Why don't you just cut it off?"

"I don't know...I was worried about it hemorrhaging." She was right. *Why didn't I just cut it off? How badly could it bleed from a small area? What did my mother know about this stuff?*

When I got home after school, I grabbed the scissors and went to the bathroom mirror. I put the scissors around the base of the wart, held my breath, and snipped firmly. The wart-and-Compound-W-string thing fell to the floor with a micro-thud, and my chin started stinging and bleeding, but nothing a little pressure couldn't stop. It was over. I had a normal chin again, except for a small open wound.

Years later, I grew another "wart," in the same spot. But this time, I knew it was a skin tag, and I removed with a nail clipper, without fear of hemorrhage. And, I stopped taking any kind of medical advice from my mother a long time ago.

ADMINISTRATIVE
CHAIRPERSON

My bullies were mostly girls. There was one boy in ninth grade who called me a cow after he thought I copied off of his sedimentary rock test, but it was a waste of effort. I never actually copied off of him, and I looked way more like a pear than a cow.

Kathy Bauer wronged me in the second grade. I had been out sick for a couple of days and returned to find a puny, institutional-mauve, plastic chair with a gray frame pushed up to my desk. I was one of taller kids, and that was not my chair. I scanned the room and saw Kathy sitting in my well-made and higher wooden chair.

I walked over and leaned in. "That's my chair. May I have it back, please?" I whispered. She was the other redhead in the class, and we probably should have been friends. But she was in the second grade popular group of girls, with their many varieties of gaucho pants—the capris of the mid-seventies. In gym class, Mr. Smith would pinch the cheeks of the cute girls—Debbie, Terri, and Kathy—but never me, even after I inflated my cheeks when we made eye contact. He just ignored me and yelled when I fouled out in kickball.

"This is *my* chair," Kathy replied, looking up at me straight in the eye.

"It's mine. You took it from my desk when I was out sick," I accused.

"No I didn't."

"You're lying. I'm telling Mrs. Sternberg." I walked over to the teacher's desk. "Mrs. Sternberg? Kathy took my chair." Our teacher, Mrs. Sternberg was a nice lady, probably in her forties, with a thick, German accent. She taught us how to count to ten in her native tongue. How delightful it must have been for her to hear twenty-two seven-year-olds shouting, "Eins, zwei, drei, vier, funf, sechs, sieben, acht, neun, zehn" in unison on a Friday afternoon.

"You don't own your chair, Jeneane. Your name isn't on it," Mrs. Sternberg explained. My name was on it, but I couldn't tell Mrs. Sternberg. I had written "Jeneane" in the upper-right corner of the back with pencil. I sulked back to my mauve seat, glancing over to visually confirm my name was still on the wooden chair. *How could someone lie like that?* I asked myself, promising eventual revenge.

Bonnie Luza was a dreadful bully. In eighth grade, she approached me while I was changing after gym class. "Can I borrow your deodorant?" she asked with phony smile on her face. I already knew she didn't like me, and I couldn't understand why she was coming to me with this request.

"I don't have any with me," I confessed, and she walked away. I didn't need to bring deodorant to gym class because I didn't smell. It would be a couple of years before I hit puberty and my armpits were odorless. Bonnie was athletic, thin, and a little taller than me, with a short eighties haircut and a perpetually sarcastic expression on her face. She was a master at dirty looks if you made eye contact with her.

"Bonnie is telling everybody you smell like B.O.," my friend Karen explained the next day. "I know it's not true."

"What?" I said. "I hate her so much. I hope she dies." About a week later, Bonnie and three of her friends approached me in the locker room after I put my gym clothes on.

"Girls just wanna have fun," they sang together in the style of Cyndi Lauper. They were laughing and kicking like the Rockettes, with their arms locked around each other's shoulders. I turned to leave for the gym. I *liked* that song. Without warning, Bonnie kicked me square and hard in the ass, and they all giggled.

"What the hell?" I gasped in pain and hurried to where the gym teacher was set up. I wanted to hurt her.

The idea of getting direct revenge on Bonnie was sweet, but I couldn't handle the possible consequences. So, I had to settle for falling asleep at night, imagining myself punching her in the face multiple times with my right fist. I also fabricated a note in disguised handwriting and left it on the floor of the girls' bathroom. It said, "Dear TJ, Guess which eighth grader has been doing the dirty deed and has a bun in the oven? Initials BL. Don't tell anyone. Sandra." Nothing ever came of it, and I went to a different school than Bonnie the next year, but I never forgot what she did. As time passed, I felt comfort in knowing that I am a kinder, better person than she is, and my life is probably happier and more fulfilling.

Eighteen years after Kathy Bauer stole my chair, I had the perfect opportunity for revenge. One day, she appeared in the entry-level training class of the office where I not only worked, I excelled. I had a college degree, a respected job, and plans for graduate school. And here, my grade school chair thief was just starting out. Truthfully, I didn't care that Kathy was there and I wished her success, but my twisted sense of humor couldn't resist.

"Oh my gosh," I gushed to my supervisor, Tracy, who I had been close to for a couple of years. "The girl who stole my chair in the second grade is in the new training class!" I told her the story.

"You know what?" Tracy said, "You should go into the training room each night and exchange her chair for a crappy one."

"That's brilliant!" I screamed. Each night, I'd slip into the training room and swap her nicer, newer black office chair for an old, wobbly tan and metal chair that was in the room. I also told my close friends what I was doing because I thought it was hilarious. Then, one day, I didn't have to swap the chairs. She had given up moving the black chair back to her desk. I had secretly won.

Eventually, I left for graduate school, and Kathy had a run of several years at her job. Then a few years ago, long after I had an established career, I stopped at a grocery store on the way home from a dentist appointment, and she was behind the register. Kathy B appeared on her name tag. She looked exhausted, her eyeliner in black circles above her cheeks. She wouldn't have recognized me. Politely and nicely, she rang me up, and I paid her. "Have a nice evening," she remarked.

"Thanks, you, too." I responded. *Poor thing,* I thought. *She looks miserable.*

I rarely think about Bonnie, but not long ago, I was reminded of her when watching a story about Nazis who immigrated to America after World War II. So out of curiosity, I found her on Facebook. I discovered she still looked about the same, with an extra fifty pounds, and her signature sarcastic smirk. There was a picture of her with her mother who had a very mean expression, and a photo of Bonnie in a cubicle. American flags and conservative posts populated her feed. Her "About Me" page said she worked for a school district in Texas, and I wanted to find out if she was a teacher, so I went to the website. She wasn't listed as a teacher, and recalling the picture of her in a cubicle, I assumed that with no college, she had some type of administrative job.

"Report Bullying Incident" was listed prominently at the top of Bonnie's school district page, so I clicked on it. A form appeared. *I wonder what would happen if I reported the bullying incident now?* I thought and looked through the form. Date of incident: About September of 1983. Who was being bullied? Me. Who was the person(s) engaged in the bullying? Bonnie Luza. What type of bullying? Physical, check. Emotional/social, check. Where did the incident take place? Gym, check. Locker Room, check. Describe what happened with as many details as possible: Bonnie Luza and her Girls Just Wanna Have Fun Rockette line teased me, kicked my flat butt, and giggled at my expense.

I could choose to identify myself and click Submit, where it said, "When you click 'Submit Form' this will be sent to the campus administrator." I assumed this was Bonnie.

Bonnie doesn't appear to have succumbed to an early death as I had wished, but there is more than a small chance that I could report her own bullying incident to her, thirty-five years later, and it probably wouldn't go unnoticed. The miracle is that I don't have to.

1984

Wade looked like a Muppet, resting his penis on the pedestal sink, in the Polaroid my brother Edward and I found in his truck. His smile was big, and his eyes were eager. We were bored one day, living on the prairie in Evansville, Wyoming, with no phone, running water, or cable TV. It was 1984, and Wade, the brother of a guy our mother worked with, left his truck on our property for a few weeks.

"Let's check the back to see if there's any liquor there," I said to Edward. It was a sunny, hot May day. Sure enough, we found four, swollen cans of Old Milwaukee and a half bottle of Bacardi rum in the bed of the truck.

"Jackpot," Edward proclaimed. "Let's check the cab." That's where we found Wade's enthusiastic dick pic. We looked at each other. "Wade," we both said with wide eyes, laughing.

Wade's brother Roland worked with my mother at the Highway Oil gas station a few miles down the road toward Casper. Earlier that week I had seen Roland leaving my mother's bedroom at five a.m., buckling his baggy, dirty pants, his hand still in a cast from when he angrily punched the desk at work. Mom's boyfriend, Ritchie with a T, was out of town visiting his mother. I was so mad when I saw Roland that morning. My mom was sleeping around, and I knew it would probably mean a new boyfriend moving in and our lives once again upheaved.

"Let's drink it," Ed said grabbing the beer and the Bacardi and heading inside. Edward was 17. He stayed in the second, smaller trailer on the property, which was connected to the main trailer by an unfinished wooden deck. Mom had stapled green, shag carpet remnants on the floors, walls, and built-in dressers of the interior. Edward was growing a single, tiny marijuana plant in one of the closets, which he nurtured from a seed. With his weekend job as a carry-out at the Safeway grocery store, Ed bought a boom box, and we listened to *When Doves Cry* as we drank our bounty.

"Mom's been sleeping with Clint," Edward revealed as he sipped one of the cans of beer.

"What? Are you kidding me?" Clint and Lorna seemed like a nice couple. They lived in a trailer a little down the road and to the left.

"I guess Clint came over one day when Mom was home and it happened," Ed explained.

"Oh, no. Is he going to move in now? What about Lorna?"

"I guess he just told Lorna that he went to get water."

Getting water was a thing in our neighborhood where digging a well cost thousands of dollars and most people had no working indoor plumbing. Highway Oil had a hose spigot where we could fill up the water containers. We would load a silver trash can and two large, black forty-gallon plastic containers onto the bed of our pickup truck, fill them with water at the gas station, and then unload them into the hallway of the main trailer where there was a third outside door.

Bathing took some planning. We had a five-gallon enamel and stainless steel pot, which we'd fill a quarter of the way and boil on the stove. Using potholders, we'd bring the pot down the hall into the bathroom and rest it in the bathtub. Then, we'd add cold water to get it to bathing temperature. Using a smaller pot, we'd scoop out some water, wet ourselves down, soap ourselves up, and then rinse ourselves off. Then, we'd dunk our head in the pot, shampoo, rinse, condition, and rinse again. The catch was, we'd have to work fast. There was a small hole in the bottom of the enamel pot that released a steady drizzle of water throughout the process.

"Jeneane, I'm out of toilet paper. Do you have anything?" Edward asked as he headed toward the outhouse, finishing his first beer.

"Yeah, I have some." Mom viewed toilet paper as a low priority expense. Once, she gave us newspaper to use, which left black ink all over our bottoms. So, I hoarded spare fast food napkins, tissues, paper towels, anything from town that could be used in a pinch if we ran out. I kept them in a zippered yellow pouch in the bathroom vanity of the main trailer, and only a few trusted people knew about my stash. It saved the day many times. "Here you go," I said, handing Ed a wad of Dairy Queen napkins.

Edward was on the swim team at the high school and was able to shower at school. I was still in the junior high and only had gym class two days a week, so I bathed at home. One day while running around the gym in my pink Trax sneakers, I heard an extra flap as my foot hit the ground, and I almost tripped. Flap, flap, as I walked. I looked down, and the sole of my shoe was peeling off, leaving only the smooth cushion behind. By the time I arrived home, my sole was almost completely detached, so I peeled it off the rest of the way. I held in my hand a perfectly intact shoe sole.

What can I do with this? I stared at it and thought deeply about how it could be useful. I went into the kitchen and grabbed the scissors. Then, I fashioned a gingerbread man-shaped figure out of the shoe sole. I drew a face with three dots and a line for a mouth. I proclaimed his name—Rubberman—and wrote a chant on the way home from the bus stop the next day:

"Who's got arms but got no hands? The Rubberman. The Rubberman."

"Who can't talk but thinks he can? The Rubberman. The Rubberman."

"Who's the best in the land? The Rubberman. The Rubberman."

Even Ed joined in on the chorus. Mom was home when we got there, and I confronted her. "I hear you've been sleeping with Clint, Mom."

"That's none of your business."

"It is my business. What about Lorna? Is he going to move in now? I'm so sick and tired of all the strange men in and out of here. There's no privacy. I saw Roland leaving your bedroom the other morning."

"What? He just came to get the keys to the station."

"Yeah, right," I said sarcastically. "I saw him buckling his pants."

"No one's moving in. Ritchie called the gas station today, and he's coming back in a couple of weeks."

"Oh, great. He's another one." I quipped.

"What's that, you're new boyfriend?" Mom asked, as I fidgeted with Rubberman.

"Who's got arms but got no hands?" I chanted.

"The Rubberman. The Rubberman." Ed returned.

"Who can't talk but thinks he can?"

"The Rubberman. The Rubberman."

"Who's the best in the land?"

"The Rubberman. The Rubberman."

"You guys are weird," Mom remarked.

To me, Rubberman was more normal than anything in my mother's world. He was hope...if you can make a flat, mini man out of the sole of tattered sneaker, and write a chant about him in one day, then anything is possible.

Rubberman hangs in my office today. I mostly ignore him, and his head detached after his now-brittle body fell to the floor, but he is a symbol of where I came from and what made me who I am...

weirdness and all.

HONEY BOO BOO

What can a fourteen-year-old do with twelve pounds of government honey? Mom brought it home from a food giveaway in Casper, Wyoming, along with five pounds of cheddar cheese, ten pounds of corn meal, six pounds of powdered milk, and five pounds of butter. We quickly found out it didn't sweeten Kool-Aid well, and other than adding it to cornmeal mush, it sat on the shelf of the small pantry in our main trailer for months.

We had been living on the prairie outside of Casper for about a year and a half. Our old trailer park landlord, Marge, sold Mom two acres of undeveloped land at the very end of Turquoise Lane, far from any neighbors. Mom and her boyfriend, Ritchie with a T, moved two trailers onto the property and arranged them in a V shape with the open end facing the road. An unfinished wooden deck connected the two trailers near the closed end of the V. We had electricity and a propane tank for heat, but no telephone or well for running water. The outhouse stood tall on the right side of the property, and our two pigs lived in a home-made pen on the hill in the back. Our un-spayed dog, Shadow, was on her third litter of puppies, nursing them in her den under the trailer.

Just my brother Edward, my younger sister Helene, and I lived at home with Mom and Ritchie. My oldest brother Kenny had moved back to New York. Derek was still in New York until his parole was over, and Desiree was in a foster home.

"Jeneane, where's Desiree?" Mom asked one night waking me from a sound sleep in the trailer park. Desiree, Helene, and I shared the same bed and room. Mom had stapled multi-colored brown, shag carpet remnants to the floor and wall of our bedroom, including the closet.

"What? I don't know. She was here sleeping last time I saw her."

"I think she went to see John," Mom said. John was a twenty-year-old guy my sister had a crush a few trailers down.

"I'm gonna go get her," Ritchie said, grabbing his shotgun. Ritchie found her at John's trailer. No one got shot, but that night, Mom took Desiree to the youth crisis center, and I wouldn't see her for another two years. Desiree had no idea we were now living in the same trailer on the prairie with a surplus of government honey.

One day, rummaging through the books on the living room shelf, I picked up *Stalking the Wild Asparagus*, by Euell Gibbons. There was a black and white close-up of a middle-aged guy's face on the cover with a stick or leaf coming out of his mouth. I flipped through the pages and read about "living off the land." There were sketches of plants and recipes, including one for dandelion wine and mead, a honey wine. The ingredients were simple and we had most of them—two sticks of cinnamon, four pounds of honey, one gallon of water, six cloves, the juice and peel of one lemon, and a teaspoon of activated dry yeast. I knew immediately that this was the destiny for the government honey. I asked my mom to pick me up a lemon and a couple of cinnamon sticks with some money I had from a babysitting job. I was excited to make wine!

"Here you go," Mom said handing me the ingredients after a trip to the store. "What are you doing with that?"

"I'm gonna try this mead recipe I found in your book."

"Mead recipe?"

"Yeah, it's honey wine."

"Oh brother. Don't make a mess," Mom warned. The next day I

hurried home after school to get started. I boiled the ingredients, as directed, and dissolved the yeast in the liquid once it cooled. I poured it into the top of a plastic cake dome—the cloves, cinnamon, and lemon peel floating freely in the mixture. I covered it loosely, and placed it in my closet to ferment until it stopped bubbling. Each day, I peeked in to see if it was still active. It gradually took on the smell of sweet Christmas vomit. After a few weeks, I sampled it, and I could taste alcohol, which thrilled me.

As the mead fermented, Mom met her future first husband at her gas station job and wasn't coming home much. I saw Ritchie around the trailers now and then, and I couldn't tell if he knew what was going on. I suspected he did, though, because he made me take down the makeshift park I built on the side of the trailer near the outhouse. I had planted a dead Christmas tree in the sand and dug a hole to make a pond with an orange hospital basin. I lined the basin with aluminum foil and filled it with water. I found an antelope femur bone and a skull and added them to the sandy grounds for decorative effect. Finally, I placed an old chair in the park so I could sit and gaze at the barren, sage brush covered landscape and dream of going back to New York.

"You gotta take down whatever that thing is on the side of the house," Ritchie instructed one day.

"Why? It's not doing anything to anyone."

"I'm gonna bring a bulldozer in here and grade the land so we can put in grass," he said.

"Is that really going to happen?" I asked. Nothing ever really got done. The well and septic never got put in; the circular driveway never got put in. The deck never got finished. It was just a piece of undeveloped property with a bunch of junk all over the place, including a huge steel tank that was supposed to be buried for water.

"Yeah, I'm doing it next week." Ritchie insisted. I begrudgingly took down the park and threw it in the garbage pit on the other side of the property. Ritchie brought home a bull dozer and flattened the area where my park was, and then the bulldozer sat there, unused.

A few weeks later, I checked the mead, and it was ready for its next phase. According to the directions, I had to bottle it, cap it tightly and store it in a cool, dark cellar for at least a month. I didn't have a cellar, and the puppies were living under the trailer. But, I did have a carpet-lined closet that was cool and dark. In anticipation of this day, I had cleaned one of my mom's large, empty Gallo Chablis bottles. I carefully transferred the contents of the cake dome into the bottle, capped it tightly, and put it in my closet.

About a week later, I came home from school, and my sister Helene was waiting for me. "Your bottle exploded in the closet, and it stinks," she revealed.

"What? Oh, no." I ran back to our bedroom, past the steel garbage can filled with our water supply, and saw the scene. She was right. The green Chablis bottle was still capped and upright, but it was in multiple pieces. The mead had leaked out and soaked the carpet. A strong stench of sweet Christmas vomit filled the room and the entire trailer. Without running water, it was impossible to clean it out of the carpet. I was upset by the stench, but even more distressed that my government mead was ruined.

"I'm moving into town with Ron and Helene. You can come with me, or you can stay here with Ritchie," my mom explained later that week. Edward was joining the army, so he wouldn't be around.

"I'm coming with you, of course." I stated, and we soon moved out. Ritchie never did plant that lawn or finish the deck, but he did dig a hole and drop in the water tank after we left. I sometimes wonder if he ever managed to get that smell out of the trailer. And, today, I have everything I dreamed of in that park—real trees, a New York lake, and a cellar with running water where I ferment my own beer—and no need for decorative antelope bones.

LOSING IT

It was the late seventies in Yonkers, New York, and Eddie O'Flaherty, older brother of my friend Christine, looked like Freddie Mercury's doppelganger. He and his tight jeans and bucked teeth had a cover band that played in front of Gimbels at Cross County Center one Saturday. "Surrender, surrender...but don't give yourself away, way," he sang, mesmerizing the young women, especially me. We made eye contact, but I knew he was out of my league.

"If you lost sixty pounds, you'd be a fox. I'd take you out," he had explained to me when I saw him at the corner store a few weeks earlier. I was there to buy some Now and Laters, he cigarettes. The candies were a good bargain...only fifteen cents, with tax.

"Really?" I said surprised. He was seventeen and I was ten. Why would he notice me?

"Yeah...you just gotta cut back on your eating for a while." Eddie looked right at me.

"Ok, I'll try," I said and hastily walked home, unwrapping my Now and Laters. I didn't believe him...he was too old and cute and wouldn't want anything to do with me. But, that was the moment I knew no boy would ever like me fat. How could I do something about it?

At thirteen, we had been living in Wyoming for about a year. I was barely over five feet tall and already one hundred-forty pounds. I couldn't stop eating bad food and was quickly outgrowing my clothes. Mom had brought me home a pair of button-fly Levi's from the defective pants bin at Target, size thirty-two waist. The defective pants got tighter and tighter by the month, causing me stomach pains and gas build-up. I wore them by undoing the buttons...first the top one, and then as I expanded, the next and the next, until only one remained fastened. Rips formed on either side of the fly where the fabric was pulled too tight by my thick body. To conceal my open fly, I wore long shirts and sweaters to school.

"Hey cow!" Chris Anderson yelled as I walked by his lunch table at junior high. I could tell he was addressing me. I wondered if my shirt was riding up and he saw my undone fly. I ignored him and kept walking with my lunch bag in hand.

"What are you having for lunch?" asked my friend Karen when I got to our table.

"Lettuce leaf," I joked. It was the first time I had brought my own lunch, and it was a salad.

"Why are you eating that?"

"Well, I'm trying to lose weight. My mom told me she followed this diet and lost thirty pounds in one week."

"What's the diet?" Karen asked, biting her bologna and cheese sandwich.

"Basically, it's a hard-boiled egg for breakfast and salad with lemon juice the rest of the day. Hopefully, I'll be done in a week." Seven days later, after sticking to the diet, I confronted my mother. "Mom, I've been following the diet all week, but I've barely lost anything."

"Your face looks thinner," Mom offered. I knew she was making that up.

"How did it work for you? How were you able to lose thirty pounds in one week?" I asked.

"I just had Kenny, so it came off pretty quickly."

"What? You just had a baby? Oh great. You've told me for years how you lost thirty pounds in one week, and it was *baby* weight? Thanks a lot, Mom." I stormed off to my room. I knew then I was going to have to figure out how to lose the weight on my own.

About a year later, and twenty-five pounds heavier, I was talking to another friend of mine about how badly I wanted to be skinny, when she warned, "Just don't take laxatives to lose weight."

"What do you mean? Why would you take laxatives?"

"It makes you poop out everything you eat. It just goes right through you, so you lose weight."

"Really? I would never do that." *This makes perfect sense,* I thought. *I'm definitely going to try laxatives to poop out my food after I eat it.*

"Mom, my stomach hurts, and I haven't been able to go to the bathroom in a while. Could you pick me up some ex-lax?" It was the only brand I knew, and the chocolate squares looked tasty in the commercials.

"Sure," Mom said. The next day, she left a box of ex-lax on my bed. I ate a couple of squares and waited for the food I overate to leave my body. After a day, nothing happened, and I took another dose. Another day went by and I took some more. On the third day, there was no activity, so I finished off the box, got dressed, and went to ninth grade at the high school. I was wearing blue jeans and a long black and white, checkered button-down shirt.

That day after lunch, I was running late, and I walk-jogged down the hall to History class clutching books to my chest. My stomach rumbled faintly, and I felt a friendly bit of gas coming on. It was nothing out of the ordinary...it was the type of gas you could stealthily let out going up or down a flight of stairs, or walk-jogging down a hallway with hundreds of other teenagers. I had no reason for concern, so I let it out.

I knew something was immediately wrong. Warm liquid effortlessly filled my underwear and started down the backs of my legs.

Oh no, I thought. *I pooped myself without even trying. What am I going to do?* I slipped into a nearby bathroom to finish the job and assess the situation.

Hiding in a stall, I wiped out my clothes with a wet paper towel as best as I could. I put another paper towel between my behind and my underwear to catch additional accidents and prevent chafing. Exiting the stall, I covered my backside with my long shirt and checked myself in the mirror. I looked normal, but sniff, sniff—I smelled like a dirty diaper.

Next, I had to figure out how to get to the nurse's office so I could go home. And the rule was, you had to have a pass from a teacher to get to the nurse. *Oh no,* I realized. *I have to go into class.* I left the bathroom and shuffled into History class, careful not to dislodge the paper towel or kick up too much wind. I pulled my teacher aside, ass away from the class.

"I just got my period," I whispered to her. Of course, I lied. I was fourteen, and I hadn't started my period yet. She gave me the pass without question.

The nurse's office had a long, turquoise, vinyl couch with some rips and cracks in it and lots of students hanging around, all trying to convince the nurse that they should go home. I sat on the couch, waiting for a pick-up, my shitty moistness soaking through my jeans and into the sofa. I could smell myself, and I hoped to god no one else could.

My brother Derek picked me up. He was nineteen and home from work at the time. He had come to stay with us after his parole was over in New York. "What happened?" Derek asked as we headed to Mom's car. I couldn't tell him I had my period because he would tease me about being a woman. And I couldn't tell him I pooped my pants because he would make fun of me for that, too.

"I peed my pants." I explained, hoping he couldn't smell me.

"What? That's fucked up, Jeneane-i. You pissed yourself? How did you piss yourself?"

"It just happened." I changed the subject, hoping nothing would soak through to the vinyl car seat. When I got home, I washed my clothes, threw out the ex-lax box, and crossed laxative weight loss off my to-do list.

NOT A MODEL

"**A**re you a model?" Dr. Stein asked while looking up at my face rash. He had asked me to stand, and at twenty-eight, I towered over his five foot frame. *Why, yes, I am a model,* I was tempted to say. I did hand-model for a "You Make the Difference" motivational poster my boyfriend, Randy, made for work. My left thumb looked pretty glamorous.

"Um, no, but thank you for asking me that. I'm an instructional designer," I explained. I knew he wouldn't know what that was, and I didn't elaborate. I just wanted to find out what was wrong with my itchy, red face. Dr. Stein pulled out a book and showed me a picture.

"Does this look like what you have?" he asked, pointing to the photo of a woman with pimples and papules around her nose, mouth, and chin.

"Yes, that's exactly it!" I affirmed, wondering how I could buy the book and self-diagnose all of my future skin disorders. This began twenty years of perioral dermatitis treatment with ointments, salves, and unguents. Eventually, I figured out that I just needed to stop using soaps and lotions around my mouth.

Being mistaken for a model with a face rash was a world away from being teased about being fat growing up. At fourteen, there was the girl in the Casper, Wyoming, library who called me "Pretty Eyes" when I entered the elevator and "Wide Ass" when I left. It was the truth. There were the boys who stood outside the high school chemistry lab and referred to me as a "4" and my friend as an "8." And, there were the siblings that dubbed me "that lazy, fat thing" and commented, "You have more rolls than a bakery." Plus, my presence was typically dismissed. I could see how people paid attention to the cuter girls, and I longed to be one of them.

So, at fifteen, I committed to my mission: becoming skinny. I had tried different methods—laxatives, Mom's baby-weight diet, riding the twelve-speed my brother Edward had bought me for my birthday, standing in front of a mirror and jiggling my blubber, but nothing was working. Buying King Size Snickers from the 7-Eleven before getting on the bus for school in the morning and locker-snacking on them throughout the day wasn't working either. I had ballooned to one hundred sixty-five pounds, and all of my clothes were tight.

That's when I devised a plan: Eat only one meal a day. Knowing school lunches were scientifically designed to be nutritionally-balanced, I made the decision to try eating those, with two percent instead of chocolate milk, and never eat the dessert. It was hard. Sometimes I would even leave a piece of uneaten bread on my tray and throw it out. This was very new to a person who always finished the food in front of her. It was easy to skip breakfast, but having no meal at night was torture. I drank water and sometimes a glass of milk if I got too hungry. Within a couple of weeks, the weight began to come off. And, I started growing taller.

"Woah, altitude," one of my tenth grade classmates said to me as we were walking down the hall at the high school.

"What do you mean?" I inquired.

"You got tall!"

"I did?" I looked up and down and realized for the first time I was about six inches taller than my friend and everyone else around. The button fly jeans that wouldn't close were loose on my waist now, and the length was hitting above my ankles. After a couple of months of blind commitment to my scheme, I had lost about forty pounds, and grew much taller, but it wasn't evident to me because I hadn't weighed myself and was wearing the same clothes.

"Mom, you gotta buy Jeneane some new clothes and get her a haircut," Edward insisted. Ed had joined the army and was sending Mom money here and there. Mom was working her gas station job at Highway Oil, and only my younger sister Helene and I were living at the house full time. It was the house I remembered most fondly in Wyoming—a green raised ranch on Sierra Vista Drive in Evansville. I had my own room on the top floor with green, shag carpet. The kitchen had a Formica peninsula with three green stools and a sliding glass door to the backyard. We had moved there with Ron Humborg, Mom's first husband, but they fought constantly, and Ron was no longer around.

"Jeneane, honey, I was able to get a credit card at J.C. Penney. I'm gonna take you to get some clothes and a haircut this weekend. Would you like that?" Mom asked one day. This was so out of the ordinary for my mother. She always cut my hair and only brought home second-hand clothes for me or ill-fitting pieces from the bargain bin. Once, she brought home two pairs of men's Lee bell-bottom jeans that were three sizes too big for me and four inches too long. Bell-bottoms had been out of style for years. "They're bootcut," Mom said.

"I can't wear these, Mom. I'll be made fun of at school. Can you take 'em back?"

"No, but I can hem them and take them in at the bottom." Mom had me model the jeans so she could measure for hemming. She then cut off the bottoms and sewed a seam down the side so they were essentially ankle-skinny jeans. Then, she washed and dried them. Although well-intended, the jeans were shrunken. They were too short and almost too tight to get my feet through. Realizing the problem, Mom trimmed the material she saved from hemming and sewed the hems back on. In 1985, when everyone was wearing Levi's 501s, I wore Lee men's haphazardly-tailored, ankle-skinny jeans, with a reattached hem at the bottom.

"Really? I would love to get new clothes. Can I get a perm?" I had tried home-perming, but my hair was a mess. I looked frumpy with baggy clothes and frizzy hair, something the mean girls at school reminded me of constantly.

"Do you comb your hair?" Natalie Langston would ask, as I would stare stoically forward, not answering her and hoping she would give up and go away.

"Natalie, you're gonna get yourself beat up," one of her hench-people would say. Little did they know, I was incapable of defending myself.

One Friday in the fall of 1985, I left school for the day looking dumpy, sad, and out-of-shape, and returned Monday morning looking like a model. Mom had made an appointment for me to get a perm at J.C. Penney that Saturday. Jason, my stylist, flirted with me as he put paper around locks of my red hair and rolled it in curlers. "I bet you would look good in a bathing suit," he said after he cut the layers in.

"I don't know," I responded with embarrassment, not realizing his intent. My hair did look amazing. It looked so good when it was done, Mom agreed to buy the special Nexxus shampoo and conditioner to keep it looking nice.

Next, I tried on all types of clothing. Staring at myself in the fitting room, I was stunned at how attractive I looked in the clothes. An intense feeling of joy welled up inside of me. Mom let me buy so many pieces—nicely-fitting Capri jeans and brightly-colored tops that flattered my shape, along with a puffy-shoulder jean jacket that complemented every outfit. She also bought me a couple of pairs of stylish flat shoes. I looked like the girls on TV in my new outfits. "Are you sure?" I would ask, as Mom told me I could buy another piece.

"Yeah, I'm sure," she would answer with trepidation. I couldn't wait to go back to school on Monday. That morning, I put on my favorite new outfit—a pair of denim capris, a vertical, pink-striped, button-down blouse, my new jean jacket, and white flats. I looked tall, thin, and beautiful.

"Who is that? Is that that Jeneane girl? What happened to her?" I heard whispered as I walked down the hallway to class.

"Oh my god, you look completely different!" Danielle Johnson from English class blurted out. She was one of Natalie Langston's hench-people a few months ago. "You look really good."

"Really? Thank you."

With my new look, people treated me differently. And, I felt like a completely new person, happier, more light-hearted, and more optimistic about my future. Boys and men who didn't know me flirted and tried to trap me into dates. The girls at high school be-friended me and asked me to hang out. Even though I knew this treatment was because of my outward appearance, I was wary but not resentful. I, too, judged myself by my appearance.

From my teens into my twenties, people approached me about modeling, and I thought about it. I even tried a couple of things, thinking I could parlay them into a writing career. But I was petri-fied of the rejection that would surely come when my leftover blubber was exposed, which is why I'm proud to say I'm an in-structional designer, not a model.

ESCAPE TO NEW YORK

I t was an easy decision to leave home at sixteen. Mom had moved my nine-year-old sister Helene and me into the musty, basement apartment of Tall Paul, the One Man Band from Wyoming. There were tiny rectangular windows near the ceiling of my bedroom that let in intermittent light. I had a TV, which I rented from an appliance store for seven dollars a week. I also had a bed, dresser, rocking chair, and a stereo, which I could use until my brother Derek and his girlfriend returned from California.

Tall Paul's one-man-band gear was set up in the living room. There was a guitar connected to an amplifier and some pedals that he could use to play chords. Two large speakers flanked the equipment. Mom covered the outside of the speakers with purple, medium-pile carpet and wrote "Tall Paul" in silver glitter on the side using Elmer's glue.

The apartment had one bathroom with only a tub. Mom bought an attachment for the tub faucet to convert it into a hand-held shower. To protect the walls from water, she applied heavy duty aluminum foil to the painted concrete surrounding the new shower with the same Elmer's glue used on the speakers.

"Who's been writing in the shower with their fingernails?" Mom asked Helene and me in an accusatory tone one afternoon. "It says, 'Natalie is my best friend.'"

"I did it," Helene confessed. She was the obvious choice. The only

Natalie I knew bullied me about the lack of variety in my pants.

"Don't do it again!" Mom swatted her on the behind for gently scratching her best friend's name into the aluminum foil shower surround and sent her to her room.

For me and my 1980s yuppie values, this basement move was a regression back into poverty. I thought we had been doing so well. We were off welfare. With her job at the gas station, Mom had actually managed to buy an above ground house. It was a clean, small, renovated three bedroom, one bath ranch in a neighborhood with families. It had running water, cable, and a phone. And no boyfriends were living with us—just me, Helene, and Mom, since Derek left for California. I took pleasure in cleaning the house, arranging the furniture into comfortable, cozy seating areas, and sitting down to gaze at what I had done. I also amused myself by performing occasional pranks.

One Friday after school, no one was home, and I was bored. I looked through the kitchen cabinets for something interesting and found a stash of bulk spices. This lady we knew had given them to us—cinnamon, nutmeg, cumin, black pepper—all in giant, restaurant-sized metal containers. *What can I do with these?* I thought. I pulled them out of the cabinet and dumped some of each into a bowl. I added flour and water and mixed it to make a brown paste. I spooned the paste into a plastic sandwich bag, cut off the corner, and squeezed it onto a saucer. It looked like a perfectly genuine pile of poop. So I put the spice poop in the refrigerator on the main shelf and waited.

The next morning, I ate my Cream of Wheat at the kitchen table with anticipation.

"Good morning," Mom said as she turned on the coffee pot.

"Morning, Mom." When the coffee was done, I watched Mom pour herself a cup, open the fridge, and add milk to her mug. She closed the fridge, took a sip of her coffee, put it down, washed a couple of dishes, and then sat down at the kitchen table, opposite of me.

"Who put puppy shit in the fridge?" Mom finally asked. I couldn't believe it. Why would someone not immediately react to a visible pile of doo-doo sitting in the refrigerator on a saucer? And, qualifying it as "puppy" shit meant Mom contemplated it enough to assume the perpetrator was a puppy, which we didn't have. Someone would have had to go out and obtain the puppy shit.

Now, we had to live with some strange one-man-band in the basement of a house that was empty. Tall Paul seemed nice enough and had a sense of humor. He was six foot five and looked exactly what I imagined Ichabod Crane to be in *The Headless Horseman*— skinny, thick glasses, and a head shaped like an oversized, sharpened pencil. Every now and then, I would put canned goods or fruit with faces drawn on them into Mom and Paul's bed. Paul would find them, giggle, and say, "Look at the face on that thing."

"I'll drive you to school," Mom said one morning out of the blue. I thought it was weird that she volunteered to do so. As we approached the school, she started talking. "I'm pregnant...due in June," she revealed.

"Oh, my God. Are you having it?" I was incredulous. How could she, at forty-two, and in deep poverty, bring another child into the world and give it a shitty life.

"Yes, I'm having it."

"I thought having another baby would kill you. Isn't that what they said after you had Helene?"

"The doctors said it's a high-risk pregnancy, but I'll be ok." I took a deep breath to process the information.

"I am not raising *your* child," I snapped. Mom pulled the car onto the shoulder in a fit of rage.

"You are my daughter and it's your duty to do what I tell you to do." I remained silent. At that moment the goal of leaving Wyoming and moving back to New York was cemented in my mind. I couldn't raise a child. I wrote to my twenty-two year-old brother

Kenny.

> Dear Kenny,
>
> How are you? I'm writing to tell you that Mom is going to have a baby in June. Her doctor says it's high risk, but she'll be ok. I'm also writing because I'm hoping to move back to New York. Can I come live with you? I figured I could move back this summer, get a job, and then finish my senior year of high school there. That way I could get in-state college tuition. What do you think? I'm very responsible and hard working. I've been saving money doing Mom's cleaning job at the movie theater. I hope to hear from you soon.
>
> Love, Jeneane

I awaited Kenny's reply. I couldn't call him because he didn't have a phone. Time went by, and Mom was seven months pregnant. She asked me to drive the car to school in case I needed to pick her up and take her to the hospital. One day, during English class, the announcement speaker beeped.

"Can you send Jeneane Walker to the office?" I knew it was my mother.

"What's wrong, Mom?" I asked her from the school phone.

"I have the worst headache in the world, and I'm not feeling the baby. Can you come get me and take me to the doctor?"

"Yes, I'll be right there." Sadly, when nurse examined her, there was no fetal heartbeat. She had miscarried. She was devastated, and I grieved for her. I also felt shame and a sick relief that another child wouldn't have to endure the pain of growing up in my mother's instability.

A couple of days later, I left a message with Kenny's friend for him to call us. He finally did. "Did you get my letter?" I asked.

"Yes, and I've been thinking about it. My girlfriend, Kim, and I are looking for a place with an extra bedroom that you could stay in."

"Really? That's awesome!" And with that conversation, life became a new adventure.

LEAVING ABNORMAL

"Y ou're not going to New York, so why don't you stop talking about it," my friend Tina Brenner challenged. I was surprised by her remark. She was one of the coolest chicks in eleventh grade in Casper, Wyoming, and we had fun together—going to high school pep rallies, squeezing through the doors at the Rocky Horror Picture Show, and just driving around in her Ford Escort. She had a short, brunette, eighties-style haircut and a knife named Mike that her rock-and-roll boy-friend had given her. They were having sex, and I hadn't yet kissed a boy.

We hung out in the basement bedroom of her parent's raised ranch, her pink shag carpet being one of my materialist fantasies. Her walls were covered with Billy Idol posters.

"What? I am going back to New York. It's all planned out. I'm gonna live with my brother Kenny so I can finish high school and get in-state college tuition," I explained. I did have it mapped out. I had been working overnight at the Eastridge mall movie theater, cleaning the lobby and bathroom, to save up for my trip. The urinals weren't the worst part of that job. Each night, I'd marvel at the creativity of the crime scene in the ladies room. But, I was slowly saving three dollars and twenty-five cents an hour so I could fly to LaGuardia airport in June, loaded with the suitcases my mom bought me for Christmas. My TV and bicycle were traveling by bus, and I was sending six boxes of random belongings by mail. My outfit would be a white pencil skirt and a short-sleeve animal print top with a black belt. I wanted to arrive in New York City in style, and I wanted Kenny to see my transformation, since I hadn't seen him in four years.

In the past eighteen months, I had gone from a chubby, short frumpy girl with ill-fitting clothes, to a five-foot-nine, slim woman with fashionably permed hair. I was having fun in eleventh grade, no longer ashamed of my appearance. Tina and I were writers. We were passing back and forth an R-rated story about how I went to New York and married David Letterman, who was my celebrity crush.

"Well I guess you could always come back if it doesn't work out," Tina decided.

Who would have thought that a little over a year later, I would be homeless.

On June 27, 1987, I got on a plane for the first time to fly from Casper to Denver to New York. I insisted on flying, despite my mother's threats.

"Mom, I'm short on the plane ticket. I was wondering if you could lend me a hundred twenty-five dollars so I can fly out of Casper? I'll get a job over the summer in New York and pay you back." Mom was in the kitchen of our basement apartment, cutting some fabric for curtains.

"Paul and I will drive you to Denver. That's a waste of money," she asserted, clearly annoyed.

"But I don't want to spend four hours in a car and then get on a plane for four hours. I'll be all wrinkled and sweaty by the time I land," I explained.

"You will do what I tell you to do." Mom came at me with the pair of scissors she was holding. She grabbed my right shoulder while thrusting the scissors toward me and held them to my face, just short of actually stabbing me.

"What the hell?" I escaped her grasp and fled into my bedroom.

Mom was taking her frustration out on me because she knew I was leaving her. She also knew I was judging her lifestyle in my attempt to make a better life for myself. I had to get out of there, so I got in touch with my brother Kenny, who agreed to lend me the money.

The flight from Casper was surreal. I said my goodbyes to Tall Paul, Mom, and my sisters, Desiree and Helene. The takeoff felt as if the plane weightlessly lifted off the ground. I watched out of the window as we flew over Casper Mountain, and the small city faded into the background. Any fear of flying was overwhelmed by the terrible prospect of having to stay in Casper.

"Kenny!" I finally spotted him waiting for me near the gate at LaGuardia. He looked mostly the same, tall, skinny, and brown. I gave him a big hug.

"I saw you walk by twice but I wasn't sure it was you," Kenny said. "You look totally different."

"Yeah, I lost a lot of weight and got tall."

"This is Kim." Kenny introduced me to his girlfriend, Kim. We were going to live in her cousin's rental house in a little town called Malden outside of Saugerties, New York.

"Nice to meet you," I said and shook her hand. She looked me up and down. I had heard about Kim from Kenny, but she didn't really seem like his type. She was more rugged than Kenny's other love interests. I looked forward to getting to know her better in this new life.

On the drive home, Kenny boasted about himself—how he was making good money in construction, how powerful his truck was, how he was going to get his silver Trans Am on the road, how the rental house was built in the 1800s and located in a neighborhood near the Hudson River. I was filled with excitement. Kenny seemed like he had his shit together.

It was close to dusk when we pulled up to the light gray, small, two story salt box. Kenny's Trans Am was sitting in the yard on blocks.

"The floor is a little slanted," Kenny said as he opened the front door to the living room. There was about a six-inch difference in height between one end of the room and the other. The carpet was olive green, and an old couch was flanked by two wooden end tables. I could see a small pile of weed, some seeds, rolling papers, and a lighter on one of the end tables.

Oh no, I thought. *They're stoners*. I had tried weed in my life and concluded it was for losers with no ambition.

"Your room is upstairs," Kenny said carrying my suitcase. I followed him up.

"This is your room. Kim's cousin gave us the bed and dresser for you to use. There's no frame, but we'll keep our eye out." My heart sank. The house and room were a step back. It was a smelly, tiny area with no closet, and I could barely stand up with the slanted ceilings. The old rug was fraying and stained. The walls were dented and marked up. Tall Paul's basement apartment in Wyoming was actually nicer.

"Thanks, Kenny." He left the room. I sat on the bed and looked around, my world shaken. *What did I just fucking do?* I asked myself. I put my head in my hands and cried. *I can't go back,* I thought. "You have to make this work, no matter what, Jeneane," I said out loud, drying my tears. I freshened up and headed downstairs to catch up with Kenny and Kim, who were enjoying some weed.

ROOMMATES

My brother Kenny and his girlfriend, Kim, weren't the only roommates I had when I moved back to New York. We had rats...lots of them. They burrowed into the Cheerios. They crawled on me while I was sleeping, startling me awake. They left rice-sized, brown turds all over the kitchen.

"Let's get 'em," Kenny said, one evening, holding a bat. He handed me a two by four, and we waited outside of the kitchen in the dark. "I can hear the little bastards. When I turn the light on, hit 'em." *Flick* went the light, and three or four rats scurried across the kitchen linoleum. Kenny sprung forth and hit one of them twice, squarely on the body—thump, thump—but it got away. I didn't get any. "Did you see that? I got 'em. I clubbed him twice," Kenny said in triumph, laughing hysterically.

"That was so messed up. There are tons of them." I gasped. I desperately wanted to move out of that house into something nicer, especially since I had just started my senior year of high school. Mom gave Kenny guardianship so I could enroll, and I wanted a place where I could bring friends over.

It wasn't long before Kenny and Kim began fighting constantly. Kenny wanted her to be more feminine. Kim was jealous that Kenny flirted with other girls. I overheard Kim insulting me to a friend of hers on the phone, and in my teenaged mind, I decided to shut her out. After a few months, we were asked to leave the house because Kim's cousin wanted to move back in. I was happy to do so, and the prospect of living somewhere without Kim was enticing. I had started working at the mall after school and was bringing some money in, so Kenny and I went looking for a two bedroom apartment that we could afford.

"Look at this place. I want to live here," Kenny said as we toured a first floor apartment on the Hudson River. It had just been renovated with new beige carpet, tile in the kitchen and bathroom, and brand new appliances. The master bedroom had double French doors that opened to a deck with a full view of the water.

"I would love to live here, but I don't think we can afford it, Kenny."

"I'll put in some overtime at work, and we can do it." I wanted to believe him, so I did, and he took the apartment for five hundred eighty-five dollars a month. I would go high school until noon, and then work the one to nine p.m. shift at the mall, giving Kenny money for the bills. On Saturday nights, my friend Tahnee and I would make twenty-five dollars taking tickets at the door of a teen dance club in Fishkill. Kim left and took her truck with her, so I bought a car from one of Kenny's friends—a 1977 Monte Carlo —orange, with a white roof. I named it Mel.

Kenny continued with his construction job, but after a few months, he was home more and more during the day, looking exhausted. Kim moved back in and seemed to be paying the bills from her job as a short order cook at Howard Johnson's. They would stay in their room some evenings, and I could hear music and loud, long sniffing noises.

"What's going on, Kenny? Are you working?" I asked one morning when he was strangely home.

"I think I have a brain tumor," Kenny said, showing me a lump the back of his head, visibly upset.

"Have you had it checked out?" I asked.

"No, I'm afraid of what they'll say. I want you to stay home Saturday night. You go to that dance club too much."

"But, it's a job. I have to go."

"No, you're not going."

"What? That's crazy. I have to go."

"If you give me some money, like a hundred dollars, to hold, I'll let you go. I'll hold it for you and give it back later," Kenny promised. So, I gave him the money and went to work that night, knowing something weird was going on. I suspected they were doing cocaine.

A few months before graduation, I was summoned to the office at the high school. "Hi Jeneane. I'm Mr. Wurzel. I'm your guidance counselor. Your grades are good. Let's talk about what you're thinking for college."

"Well, I want to go, but I don't know if I can afford it. I might have to work for a year first."

"Let's put in an application to Ulster anyway and fill out a financial aid form." Ulster was the local community college that everyone referred to as thirteenth grade. "I'm gonna need some information from your parents. Can you get that?"

"I live with my brother. He's my legal guardian. I don't think I'm gonna get any financial aid because he makes too much money."

"Well let's just see..." And so, Mr. Wurzel filled out the forms for me. Months went by. The day of my high school graduation in late June of 1988, I put on a white leather miniskirt and high heels, donned my semi-translucent white cap and gown, and headed to the ceremony. Kenny, his girlfriend, Kim, my boyfriend, Will, and my friend Tahnee were in attendance. The next morning, I was awoken by loud, constant banging. Bam, bam, bam, bam, bam.

"Get the fuck out here, Kenny!" A man was yelling at the front door. "You haven't paid rent in six months, and I want you out of here, now! I've got the Sheriff coming with an eviction notice." It was the landlord, Mr. Leighton.

Six months? I thought. *Oh my god...I've been paying him the whole time. He's been snorting the money.* I quickly got dressed, but Kenny wouldn't come out of his room. The Sheriff and the landlord broke into the house, only to find Kenny in his room naked. The Sheriff ordered him to get dressed and leave immediately with all of our belongings. Mel could only hold so much, so we put all of our furniture in the front yard. A friend of Kenny's let us stay at his house until we could figure out what to do. There we were, homeless, the day after I graduated high school.

"What the hell happened to the money, Kenny?" I confronted him in the living room of his friend's house.

"I did pay him. I don't know what he was talking about. I was only a month behind. We can look for a cheaper place." Kenny said.

"What? There is no way I am moving in again with you, Kenny. I can't trust you." That remark seemed to affect Kenny deeply, and we barely spoke for months. He remained essentially homeless for a year, sleeping on people's couches, until he joined the Navy.

I turned eighteen that summer, finally able to take care of myself. I moved into a cheap studio apartment in Woodstock with my first boyfriend, Will, and commuted to college. And because my mother gave up custody of me, I received financial aid as an independent student—enough to cover my tuition, books, and an inexpensive car after Mel broke down. I also began a job working evenings with steady pay and health insurance.

Things slowly became normal. It was only after leaving my family that I could progress toward the life I wanted for myself. Despite the dark time in his mid-twenties, Kenny eventually made a great life for himself. Today, I couldn't ask for anything more. My only wish is for the continued happiness and health of the people I love.

FATHER FIGURE

According to official government records, my father was a blank. The "FATHER" area on my birth certificate was empty. The assortment of men Mom brought home to live with us over the years hardly filled the void. There was the Croatian waiter, Lenny, who was a great cook and a nice man but smelled like B.O. and told us to "wacuum the floor" in his thick accent. Mom put deodorant on the couch where he rested his armpit. There was Tom, my younger sister's father who was abusive, and then Jerry. There was Nick, Richie without a T, Ritchie with a T, Ron, and Tall Paul, the One Man Band from Wyoming, plus a number of other men with names like Jamie, Jamesy, Sam, and Clint who were just passing through.

I had two clues as to who my father was: My mother had written his full name and social security number in her address book, which I memorized: Robert Coppola. And I had a waist-up picture of my mom hugging and kissing my father, from about 1970. He was wearing a chartreuse, short-sleeved, button-down shirt and had sideburns and curly brown hair that hit in the middle of the back of his neck. I could see only his left ear and the part for his comb-over, which swooped right. Mom was wearing a sleeveless, orange-flowered top, and her hair was in ringlets from rollers and golden in the light. The backdrop, a wall oven.

Since my late teens, I had made a few attempts to track down Bob Coppola. Phone book, police officer friend, writing to the Red Cross from an address I found in a Dear Abby column, the internet, but nothing was successful. I had fleeting fantasies about who he was…maybe he was wealthy, maybe he was part of the mafia, maybe he was related to Francis Ford Coppola, but my hopes were low.

In 1995, the internet started working better. One day, I typed in my father's social security number and turned way to make some notes. When I glanced back at my screen, there it was in green lettering on a black background: Robert Coppola, Commack, NY. Wife: Mariana. Two sons: Joseph and Salvatore. I knew it was him.

A hand-written letter seemed like the right way to infiltrate my father's life. I had no idea if he would even want to bother with me. With a phone call, I could get the wrong person or someone could hang up on me. I could show up at the front door, but that could be slammed in my face. I wouldn't be able to take that kind of rejection. A letter would give him time to process and tell his family, and then he could decide if he wanted to contact me. For me, I was kind of numb and ready for anything.

After a few practice runs, the letter went like this:

Dear Mr. Coppola,

My name is Jeneane Walker, and I am your daughter, born to Helene in 1970. You're probably quite startled by this letter, but this seemed to be the best way to contact you after more than twenty years. I would be very pleased to meet you.

I have an apartment in Kingston, NY, and I work evenings at an insurance company and some days as a substitute English teacher, waiting for a position to open. My mother, Helene, is well and living in Louisiana.

I do not wish to change or interfere in your life in any way, but I would like to meet and get to know you. Please feel free to contact me by phone at 845-338-8197. I look forward to hearing from you.

Sincerely,

Jeneane

I mailed the letter on Wednesday and took a spontaneous trip with my boyfriend to visit my brother Kenny for the weekend. Kenny lived in suburban Philadelphia, stationed there with his wife and daughter as a Navy Seabee. He and Rebecca lived in a raised ranch and were having a barbeque with Kenny's Navy buddies when we arrived.

"Let's go four-wheeling," Kenny said to me and his Navy friends, taking a drag of his cigarette and flicking it away. He was met with a resounding, "YEAH!" His group of military buddies was macho and gung-ho.

Kenny's four-wheeler was a red and white Ford Bronco, designed to four-wheel to the grocery store, school, and back. I jumped in the front seat, and my boyfriend, Randy, got in the back as Kenny drove us into the woods behind his house and immediately into a stream, where the Bronco stalled in four feet of water. Kenny tried the ignition several times but it wouldn't start.

"Stay here," he said. "I'll get this pulled out in a minute." I climbed into the back seat with Randy as the water filled the bottom of the Bronco and bubbles broke on the surface—bloop, bloop, bloop. Randy and I looked at each other and giggled. We weren't in danger yet, and we were excited for the action.

Kenny went to get help from his friends. The Bronco was half-in and half-out of a calm but deep stream, tilted with its left side in the air. The woods were bucolic, with sun shining through a canopy of trees and what appeared to be a trail through the vegetation. Just then, a convoy of men on four ATVs drove through. They all stopped, got off their ATVs and stood, staring at us silently. They didn't ask if we needed help or a ride. They just soaked in the scene. One gentleman put his hand in his black sweats and began moving it around his private area for many minutes. He had the concentration of a baby who had found its belly button for the first time. None of his friends noticed or protested. Randy and I looked at each other in disbelief.

"What the hell is going on," we said to each other. Our gradual descent into a watery grave was being witnessed by some ATV guy quietly exploring his junk in the Pennsylvania woods. "This is how it ends, isn't it?" Randy joked.

Kenny returned with one of his buddies, and we jumped out of the Bronco to dry land, feeling a bit safer. The Bronco was towed out, but the engine needed replaced and his wife was not happy.

"I found my father," I said to break the tension back at the house. "Do you remember anything about him?" Kenny was six years older than me, so "Bob Coppola" was one of Mom's boyfriends to him.

"Not really," Kenny said. "Just that he had a comb-over and a pocket protector with pens coming out of it."

When we returned to my apartment the next day, my answering machine light was blinking in earnest, inviting me to press play.

BEEP FOR THE WAIT

How do you prepare to hear your father's voice for the first time? I was twenty-four and had no memory of the visits that stopped when I was eighteen months old. He was this guy named Bob Coppola who met my mom at a cocktail lounge near LaGuardia airport in 1969. She was bartending, and he seemed lonely, at least according to her story.

Now, I had just returned home from a weekend away after locating Mr. Coppola and writing him a letter, and he must have opened it, read it, and called my apartment, as I had suggested. This was real. My boyfriend, Randy, and I sat down in the living room as if we were about to have a serious talk about our relationship. I took a deep breath and pressed play on the answering machine.

Hang up number one. Beep. Hang up number two. Beep. Hang up number three. Beep. Hang up number four. Beep. Hang up number five. Beep. Then, finally a message in a deep, stammering, adult male voice with a Long Island accent:

> Uh, hi, Jeneane. I guess this is the guy you haven't seen in uh, twenty-two-and-a-half years or so. I was trying to get a hold of you. I'll leave you my uh beeper number and you call me back. It's uh 631-829-5297. Okay, talk to ya, bye.

I looked at Randy. "Oh my God, how does a beeper number work?" I asked.

"I don't know."

After all of these years, my first contact with my father, Bob Coppola, would be initiated by a beeper, and I had never used one before. I dialed the number and heard a loud tone. Startled, I immediately hung up. I dialed again and punched in my phone number. My phone rang back almost immediately, and I answered. Randy disappeared into the bedroom to give me some space.

"Hello?"

"Jeneane? Well hi, there."

"Hi, how are you?"

"I thought it was you when I saw someone called with no number."

"Yeah, I wasn't sure how it worked. I'm really glad to hear from you," I said. "What are you like?" It's curious how little of the conversation I remember. I learned he worked in IT at Reuters. He had a wife, Mariana, from Columbia, and two sons, Joe and Sal, who were few years younger than I was. His wife knew about me but the boys didn't. I told him about my life, my job, my boyfriend, applying to graduate school. We talked about medical stuff. He had post nasal drip, lactose intolerance, and a heart attack in the late eighties. I was a good sleeper and hated my alarm clock for the deep, low, menacing tone it made when it sounded, and how it regularly malfunctioned and made me late when I snoozed it. He said he wanted to come up and meet me in person, so we set a date for the coming Saturday. I gave him directions to my place, and we hung up.

"How'd it go?" Randy asked.

"It went fine. He seems normal. He's gonna come up and spend the day on Saturday." My brain struggled to process the encounter. What was it like to have a father who cared about you, commented on who you dated, gave you spending money, worried about whether you got home safely? It was all very strange to me. When I was in third grade in Yonkers, New York, Mrs. Dodd passed out construction paper, scissors, and crayons, and instructed us all on how to make a tie-shaped Father's Day card for our dads. I went up to her desk. "I don't have a dad," I explained.

"Yes, you do."

"No, I don't."

"Yes, you do. Now, get back to your desk and make the card."

She was annoyed. I made the tie-shape out of orange paper, drew diagonal stripes on the front, and wrote inside, "Happy Father's Day. Love, Jeneane." When I got home, I showed it to my next-door neighbor friend Maureen. "Can you use this with your dad?"

"Yes," she said, and crossed out my name, put hers, and gave it to her father.

Saturday finally came. I was excited for my father to see my one-bedroom apartment. It was bright and had brand new beige carpet and freshly painted white walls. The kitchen was harvest gold and outdated but clean, and it had a dishwasher. There was a stackable washer-dryer in the hall closet and a fireplace in the living room, perfect for burning Duraflame logs or unwanted mail. From the living room window, I could see the grass and sidewalks in the courtyard and the rock under the tree where the next year, my brother Edward would find out his wife wanted a divorce.

I had cleaned my apartment top to bottom and left a New Yorker magazine on the kitchen table with my pair of Harry Potter-style glasses on top, in case he couldn't tell I wore contacts. The stage was set hours in advance for him to see that I was normal and not scary. All I needed to do was wait.

Sitting patiently in the living room, I thought about how I could break the tension. Should I poke arm and leg holes into a Hefty bag and wear that like a California Raisin? Black out a tooth? Put on a fake neck tattoo? Take my Filipino friend's offer and have her answer the door? It didn't seem real...it felt more like I was directing a scene that I had control over. This unsuspecting man was about to meet his daughter, and she was orchestrating the experience.

Ding dong. I went down the stairs to the front door and opened it. Standing there, looking right at me, was Bob Coppola. "Hi, how are you? I'm Jeneane. It's great to see you." I knew immediately that I shared half of the DNA of the person in front of me. My father was about my height and had a belly. He no longer had the comb-over. He was mostly bald with brown hair on the sides and back of his head. He had my eyes and several one or two-inch hairs growing straight out between his eyebrows at the top of his nose. He wore a white, button-down, short-sleeved shirt with a pocket protector, where he stored a pen and his reading glasses.

After an awkward hug, I said, "Come upstairs. How was the drive?"

"I have something for you." Bob Coppola said, handing me a gift.

"Oh my gosh. Thank you...you didn't have to do that. Should I open it?" It was a small rectangular box, about the size of a hard cover novel, that was wrapped in pretty rose-patterned paper and had a flower bow, which I could tell was hand-woven out of the same paper.

"Yeah, go ahead."

"It's beautifully wrapped."

"My wife, Mariana, wrapped it." I carefully unwrapped the box to preserve the paper and bow. Inside was a new Sony alarm clock radio with a sleep timer.

"Oh wow! This is so great. Thank you so much."

"It was the only thing I knew you needed." He was right. I wanted to make sure he knew I wasn't asking anything from him but a relationship.

I gave him a tour of the apartment, and we sat in the living room and got to know each other. I found out his mother was ninety-three and in a nursing home with a broken hip. He was a New York Giants season ticket holder. He met his wife about the same time he stopped coming to see me. She didn't speak much English, and although he showed her photos, which he could no longer find, he wasn't sure she understood. Around that time, my mother said she was going to marry her boyfriend, Richie with no T, who was a nice guy, so he thought Richie would be my father and I would be okay. He asked me about my older brothers and sister, who he knew when he lived with us for about a year.

And then he drove us to dinner at an Italian place, and we chatted some more. He taught me the word zeppole for the fried dough balls with powdered sugar the restaurant served. He told me we were Italian Calabrese, from Calabria in Italy. And then he dropped me off at my apartment and said he would call me the next week after he talked to his wife. He wanted me to meet her and the boys, at some point. I was excited for this new life adventure.

He called a week later and we talked. A couple more weeks passed, and the phone rang. He sounded nervous. "I'm calling to tell you I'm sorry, but I'm going to have to *suspend relations* with you." It seemed like he was doing IT work. I imagined a dialog box blinking "Suspend Relations" in his mind.

"What do you mean? What's going on?"

"My wife is upset and crying all the time. She's talking about divorce. I'm going to get her some counseling and I'll get back in touch when things are better. Okay?"

"Um. But, I was enjoying getting to know you, and I like you."

"I'm sorry. I'll call you back when things calm down...probably a couple of months. Bye."

"Okay, bye." I said breathlessly.

I hung up, stunned. Didn't I show him how normal I was? The tears should have come, but they really didn't. I hadn't fully processed having a father, so losing a father couldn't hurt me. I knew I had done nothing wrong...I just existed. I wasn't asking for anything except a relationship. I went on with my life and pretended not to care about his next call.

BIRTHDAY CAKE

On the morning of my twenty-fifth birthday, I woke up with an itinerary I did not expect. There would be no celebrating with friends, rum and diet cokes, or karaoke. It was late summer. I was taking a train to Grand Central to meet my father's family on Long Island for the first time. Relations had been *unsuspended*.

A couple of months earlier, a breakdown in negotiations had occurred. My newly-found father's wife needed counseling to deal with my sudden reappearance into his life. In the meantime, he said he had to *suspend relations*.

My father called in late-July to let me know his wife, Mariana, was feeling better with some counseling, and she wanted to speak with me. "She'll call you in the next day or so," he said.

The phone rang later that evening.

"Jeneane, this is Mariana. I'm so happy to talk to you." Her Columbian accent was somewhat soothing. "I had a dream about you and your mother. You were struggling. I have visions...I have dreams, and I want to tell you I am sorry. I pray for you every day. I pray and pray. Please come to visit. You are welcome here anytime."

"Oh, thank you. You don't know how much I appreciate that." This was certainly what I wanted to hear, but I was guarded. Was she sincere? Would relations be suspended again?

She handed my father the phone. "I was thinking you could come down on your birthday and stay the night," he suggested. "I'll pick you up at Grand Central. Joe and Sal will be here."

"Do they know about me?"

"Not yet. We're gonna tell them this weekend." My father knew I had my birthday off from work. During one of our phone calls, I had told him how much I loved my birthday, and I never worked on it, if I could help it. I disliked being the center of attention, but my birthday was the one day I wanted special treatment—dinners out, hats, cake, singing, and fun.

"Yeah, that sounds great! I'm excited to meet everyone." I was excited and terrified. What if my brothers didn't want to meet me? What if this was a trap? Get the bastard daughter into our home and tell her she is worthless and unwanted on her favorite day. It didn't seem likely, but it was my irrational fear.

The train ride down to Grand Central seemed never ending. Would my brothers like me? Would we have anything in common? Would their house smell funny? Would I be able to go to the bathroom in private? The train pulled into the station, and I hopped off with my overnight bag. I was wearing a pair of light colored Levi's and a tucked in white, sleeveless button-down shirt with a black belt. I had bangs. My friend Maria, who worked in the MetLife building, came downstairs and met me in the main concourse for moral support.

"Happy Birthday," she said, and gave me a hug.

"We need to keep an eye out for…" Just then, my father walked up wearing beige Dockers shorts with white socks pulled up his calf.

"Hi, this is my friend Maria. She works upstairs. Maria, this is my father, Bob Coppola." They exchanged greetings and we headed to the car. A young man emerged, took my bag, and put it in the trunk.

"Jeneane, this is Sal."

"Hi Sal, nice to meet you." I gave him a hug. Sal just found out he was my little brother, and I wanted to get to know him. He had dark brown hair and eyes and seemed shy. He didn't look much like me, and he was clearly into body building. As my father drove, I asked Sal lots of questions. He was attending Hofstra University, as a business major. We both went to Woodstock '94 and the same Metallica and Guns 'n Roses concert in '93. "You know, since you're younger, you have to listen to me," I joked. He responded with an awkward giggle.

After about thirty minutes, we pulled up to a two-story colonial built in the seventies. Mariana and Joe greeted me warmly with a hug. Mariana was an attractive woman in her fifties, a little over five feet tall, with long brown hair and brown eyes, and a kind smile. Joe was slightly shorter than I was and looked like me in the face, with dark brown, short hair and brown eyes. He was also into body building and seemed very outgoing.

As my brothers gave me a tour of the house, I thought, *This is the home I could have grown up in*. There was an in-ground pool in the backyard filled with dark water. Ducks used it sometimes. Joe and Sal shared a small room upstairs. There was a twin bed on each side, and the floor was completely covered in stacked CDs, VHS tapes, games, books, and clothing, chest high. You could take only about two steps into the room before it swallowed you. It was a disaster. "We actually cleaned this," Joe said. We both laughed. He knew it was ridiculous. It was a mansion compared to the trailer with no running water, phone, and sometimes, no heat that I spent some of my teenage years in.

In a few minutes, dinner was served. The dining room had a large, ornate wood table. They sat me at the end, and my father sat to my left. Mariana sat to my right. We ate chicken parmesan, baked ziti, and salad. The sauces were chunky with tomatoes and homemade, and I ate excessively. My father was quiet as I led the small talk with my brothers and Mariana.

After dinner, a cake appeared in front of me with two lit candles, a two and a five. "Happy Birthday to you," they sang and handed me a small gift. It was a twenty-four karat gold Figaro chain necklace. I put it on, they stood around me, and we posed for pictures—clearly their birthday ritual. I felt as if I were a tourist attraction being visited by a kindly family of four.

We then moved into the TV room where my father and Joe showed me home videos of Joe and Sal growing up. They were usually wearing capes, running around lawlessly shooting each other and pretending to die horrible deaths. I calculated that I was probably eight at the time of the videos and living in Yonkers with my five other siblings, Mom, and Tom, my sister Helene's dad. I wondered what the purpose was. *Why show an abandoned daughter scenes of what she didn't have? Did they see how fortunate they were to have a video camera? To be running around in capes and being carefree?* I laughed and commented and made small talk until my eyes grew heavy for sleep.

"I'll show you to your grandmother's room," my father said. Annette Coppola was ninety-three and in a nursing home after breaking her hip. I knew nothing about her, and she didn't know about me. I wanted to ask if I could see her, but I was afraid it would scare my father away, since I thought she likely wouldn't accept me. Her room had a twin bed, a tall dresser with a doily on top, and a framed photo of my grandmother on the side table. I stared at her picture and waited for something spiritual to happen before I fell asleep. Nothing did.

I woke the next morning and listened for people roaming about the house so I could avoid awkward encounters. It was completely silent. I crept into the hall bathroom to brush my teeth and use the facilities. There were purple and pink pastel striped towels hanging on the racks that were so new, they seemed to soak up no water—they left lint on my wet skin after I brushed my teeth.

I went to use the toilet, and stood there, frozen. There was a large stewed tomato stuck to the side just under the rim. My stomach was usually strong, but I couldn't bear the thought of how it got there. I flushed the toilet several times to get it to go away, but it wouldn't move. I could have used a toilet brush, but the idea made me even more sickened. I physically had to leave it there. All I could imagine is that one of my new brothers would find it and tell their friends about their surprise sister who poops out whole stewed tomatoes. *It's not my tomato!* I thought. *It's not my tomato!* I showered and went downstairs, leaving the tomato behind.

"We wanted to take you to East Northport for lunch. It's a nice town on the water with shops and restaurants. How does that sound?" My father asked.

"That sounds like fun," I said. My father, Sal, Mariana, and I drove to East Northport for lunch and then walked around until it was time for me to leave for the train. We chit-chatted, stopped to look at stores and took in coastal views. I became the leader, making the decisions about where to go, what to look at, what was exciting. This sweet family moved passively as a unit as I directed their experience. I started to realize Bob Coppola preferred to "go with the flow."

"When are you going to call me Dad?" my father asked as he dropped me off at Grand Central.

"I'll call you Dad." I said, giving him a hug and kiss. On the one hand, I was relieved I could say, "Hi Dad," and no longer had to avoid referring to him. On the other, was he really a dad to me?

On the ride home, I stared out the window, still processing. There was no rule book for what I had just experienced. I had been rejected, and then accepted. They were nice people with a life story very different from mine. Would they make an effort to see me again? Was I part of the family? I wasn't sure.

Over the next thirteen years, I would see my dad in person only six more times.

THE WEDDING PARTY

The morning of September 11, 2001 in upstate New York was gorgeous and routine. I slipped a luxurious purple bathrobe over my nightgown and sat down in my home office to start work. Curiously, my colleagues in Hartford, Connecticut, were listed as "Unavailable" in the instant messaging service we used.

My business phone rang. "Hello. Jeneane speaking."

"Are you okay?" my boyfriend, Randy, asked, sounding very concerned. He was at a planning meeting for work in St. Louis.

"Yeah, why, what's up?"

"Turn on the TV," Randy pleaded.

I was almost grateful that my brother Derek wasn't alive to see the heartbreaking and terrifying events of that day. His surprising death a month ago meant anything crazy could happen, including this. One evening a few weeks earlier in August, I got the call.

"Derek OD'd," my younger sister Helene said. "Edward found him on the couch when he came back from his honeymoon with Christina." She was crying.

"What? Oh no. No, no, no, no. What happened? Was there a note?"

"No. Edward just came home and found him."

"Oh my god, Helene. He fucking did it. Does everybody know?" I asked, barely able to speak. Derek had attempted suicide at least once after his last breakup, and many times over the years. Now he finally went through with it after the chaos of Edward's wedding night.

"Desiree and Mom know. I don't think Kenny knows. Can you call him?"

"Oh shit, Helene. Yeah, I'll call him." I had to process several minutes before calling Kenny. I had just said goodbye to him a few days earlier in Wyoming after a whirlwind of wedding celebrations and arrests. I had flown home to New York while Derek awaited his court hearing in Casper for a felony assault charge.

Things had been building the week of the wedding. A couple of hours before the rehearsal dinner, I was at my sister Desiree's house talking to Derek about his ex-girlfriend. He showed me a small 7up bottle full of clear liquid, poured some into a shot glass, and drank it.

"What is that?" I asked.

"It's GHB," Derek revealed.

"The date-rape drug?" I was incredulous. "Why the hell do you have that?"

"It makes me feel mellow. I took it in my carry-on," Derek revealed. "I brought this in my shoe." Derek held up a small bag of white powder.

"What's that?" I asked.

"It's cokeyainne!" Derek proclaimed in a Scarface-like accent. Derek was into some serious, reckless shit—taking risks he shouldn't, doing drugs he shouldn't—a ticking time bomb. It was hard to believe we once were close.

When I was fifteen, still living in Casper, Wyoming, I was tall enough that I passed for the drinking age of nineteen. Derek would take me with him dancing, to bars, and to underground, after hours dance clubs. He had fun, welcoming friends, Pizalle, John, and Stevie, who he met playing basketball at the local rec center. They took me under their wing and made sure no one messed with me. One night, we met at Pizalle's house before going out, and I saw someone light rock on fire inside a glass bowl and inhale the smoke. "What the hell is that?" I asked Stevie, who was a little older than me.

"You don't know what that is?" Stevie asked in disbelief. "Come on, you know what that is."

"No, I have no idea. Is it a drug?"

"Yeah, it's cokeyainne!" Stevie explained. "I don't touch that stuff."

That night, as we were dancing to the SOS Band at the Jammin' Manor, an after-hours dance club, a man whispered in my ear. "Can I go home with you tonight?"

"What?" I asked.

"Can I go home with you tonight?"

"Um, no." I responded. "I'm here with my brother," I shared and quickly ran over to Derek.

Derek was usually the biggest, loudest guy around—tall, dark, and considered handsome by all of the women. When Derek sneezed, it was so loud, the house would shake. At his best, he was funny, charismatic, witty, and popular, and he loved the attention. When he was in that state, I was proud to be around him, and I knew he would take care of me. But it was like walking on eggshells. Derek could get set off by the slightest thing and make life miserable for everyone. It usually involved him feeling like a victim and that nobody cared about him.

That Easter when I was fifteen, my mom, Helene, Desiree, Derek, and I sat down for dinner. Derek had sprained his ankle playing basketball the week before at the rec center and was spewing negativity, hobbling around with a cane and a boot on his foot and complaining about everything. "I hate this fucking town and everything in it." I knew that, in his mind, he thought we all should be paying more attention him and doing things for him because he was hurt.

"We're just trying to sit down for a family dinner," Desiree said.

"Family? This is no family. This is a zoo!" Derek yelled. Then, he picked up his plate of food and threw it across the table, past my sister, and into the wall. He didn't calm down until the police came.

By the time we were back in Casper together for Edward's wedding, Derek and I hadn't spoken in seven years, and he was a mess. He had come to visit me from Staten Island seven years earlier with a Navy buddy of his. After a night dancing and drinking with "Fun Derek" at local bars, we went back to my upstate New York apartment to go to sleep. Derek, six-foot-four and hungry, raided the fridge of anything edible.

"You going to make us breakfast in the morning, Jeneane-I?" Derek asked.

"Sure, if you can throw a couple bucks my way." I was scraping by. Overtime was cut at work, and I was barely making my bills. To feed two grown men was going to cost me a lot of money, and this was the second weekend in a row he had stayed with me.

"After all I do for you, you ungrateful little fucking bitch? You ask me for money for breakfast? I don't ever ask you for anything." Derek continued to yell his resentment at me in a scary, violent way, ready to assault me. His Navy buddy begged him to calm down and protected me from getting physically hurt.

"I'm low on money, Derek."

"I don't give a fuck, you petty bitch. I come up here to visit you, and you ask me for money?"

I truly didn't understand where his rant was coming from—he was erratically set off. Later on, I put some of the puzzle pieces together that helped explain it, but wasn't an excuse. He had just split with his girlfriend, and a close friend of his—a father figure to him—had died a few days earlier, plus the alcohol. But, I knew that was the end of it. I needed to cut him out of my life. I was an adult, out on my own, free of the family bullshit, and he brought it back into my world. The next time I saw him was seven years later in Wyoming before the wedding.

"Hi, Scum. You look great!" I said and hugged my brother Edward tightly after I got off the plane in Casper. We nicknamed each other "Scum" after a campy TV show from the eighties.

"This is my fiancé, Christina." A petite, pretty brunette in her twenties approached me with her hand out smiling—a fully rotten set of teeth revealed themselves. They looked caked in baked beans.

"Hi, nice to meet you," I said shaking her hand and keeping my composure. I thought, *If my brother Edward loves her, there has to be something special here.*

Just then, my brother Derek walked up behind me, having just deplaned from his flight. "Hey, Mr. Foyd!" Derek gave Edward a bear hug. Mr. Foyd was Derek's nickname for Edward. I had no idea why. "Hey Jeneane-I." Derek gave me a light hug and looked over my shoulder at Christina, who was smiling.

"Oh, hell no!" Derek exclaimed, and jumped several feet back after taking one look at Christina's wide grin. Christina burst out laughing and popped a set of fake Billy Bob teeth out of her mouth showing off her perfect smile. That seemed to set the stage for a fun, lighthearted week.

"We going to see a hitchin'," I said to my sister Desiree as she drove us to the wedding a few days later. "We need some banjo music." This was Edward's second marriage, and we were excited for him. When we drove up to the church, my mother and my younger sister Helene were already there. Edward, Derek, and Kenny showed up about a half hour late with the best man. I could tell they had all been partying.

"I now pronounce you husband and wife." And just like that, Edward and Christina were married. The reception was fun and up-beat...absolutely perfect. We were on a high...it had been twenty years since all of my brothers and sisters and my mother were together in one place. No one wanted the party to end.

"We're headed to the Beacon Club. Pass it on," Edward shared. Most of the wedding party, the family, and many of the guests headed to downtown Casper, in our wedding clothes, and we danced and drank until closing at one a.m.. I walked outside and saw Derek in his tuxedo talking to a cop.

"Hey man, we're just trying to have a good time," Derek explained.

"What's going on?" I asked a fellow wedding guest who was watching.

"The cop was trying to arrest one of Christina's cousins for peeing on the sidewalk, and Derek is trying to get him out of it."

Oh no, I thought. Just then, the cop yelled, "Get down," and attempted to tackle Derek, but Derek was too strong and tried to get away. A second cop came over to restrain Derek as eight more cop cars pulled up. The guy who peed on the sidewalk fled into the night. Two officers wrestled Derek to the ground in the middle of the street, face down on the pavement. A third officer hurried over and soaked his face in mace. I stood on the sidewalk and watched helplessly, pulling out my Vivitar film camera and taking pictures. Derek was completely subdued, in cuffs in the middle of the road, his eyes burning, when another officer went to his K-9 vehicle, retrieved a German Shepherd, and commanded it to bite Derek's leg.

"What are you doing? He didn't do anything!" I yelled at the cop, snapping pictures. The cop ignored me and stood guard as the dog gripped Derek's thigh, shaking its head. Derek screamed in pain and struggled to get the dog off of him.

Just then my sister Helene ran up, "You can't do that. He's my brother," she screamed. Another officer grabbed her and put her in cuffs while saying, "You're under arrest for interfering with an officer." Snap, snap. I continued taking pictures.

Meanwhile, my brother Kenny, an active Navy officer questioned the cops. "I'm in the military. My brother didn't do anything. What's going on?" Kenny, six-foot-six, brown and skinny, in a gray suit, was hastily arrested for interference, doused in mace, and stuffed into a police car. Luckily, Edward and his new wife had gone home for the night, as did my sister Desiree and her boyfriend, Bart.

I stood there on the sidewalk as the police took three of my siblings to the local jail, Derek and Kenny in intense pain. I pulled out my 1998 Motorola cell phone. "Hi, Mom. You're not going to believe this."

We managed to bail them all out by morning, Derek being charged with a felony for assaulting the German Shepherd officer, and Helene and Kenny with a misdemeanor for interfering with the conduct of the police. This meant Derek couldn't leave town before his court hearing the following week. He stayed at Edward's house while we all flew home. A couple of days later, Edward found him.

"We gotta clean out his apartment," Edward said to me on the phone. It was a way for us to be useful, to do something, together, while we awaited the autopsy results and the funeral. My mother had requested an out-of-state medical examiner because of the dust-up with the cops, and his death so soon afterward.

Derek was unattached. He had a thirteen-year-old son who lived in Ohio with his mother, a small one-bedroom apartment in Camden, New Jersey, and a Ford Probe. Edward bought a flat-bed trailer in Wyoming and drove to New Jersey, while I drove down from New York. Helene flew in from California, and Kenny drove up from Mississippi.

At the apartment, it was disturbing to see how Derek lived. It was in complete disarray...clothes strewn about and some empty spaces in closets and drawers where his ex-girlfriend had recently cleaned out her belongings. In his living room, he had taken the cushions off the couch, lined them up length-wise on the floor, and put a fitted sheet over them for a makeshift bed. "It looks like Derek was sleeping there." I said to Edward. "I wonder if he couldn't sleep in his own bed after the breakup."

"That's mine!" my sister Helene announced, pointing to an eighties-style mauve and black piece of wall art with a brass frame. She idolized Derek. In her mind, he was a saint. She hadn't seen him physically overpower Desiree and Mom, or how he mistreated his girlfriends. She'd never been on the receiving end of one of his sincere, anger-filled death threats. I spotted the only thing I wanted. It was an unused, translucent, oval bar of soap with a skinny green plastic alien suspended inside. In my mind, Derek must have been having fun when he bought it or somebody gave it to him. It represented good times, and that's how I wanted to remember him.

We put the Ford Probe on the trailer, piled on his furniture and anything salvageable, and Edward, Kenny, and Helene drove back to Casper. I flew out soon after for the funeral.

A few weeks later, the autopsy results arrived. Derek, aged thirty-five, died of pneumonia, not drugs. There were pot, cocaine, methadone, and other drugs in his system, but they didn't do him in. Desiree recalled he wasn't feeling well that day and threw up several times. After self-medicating, he must not have realized what grave danger he was in, probably from the mace.

A local Casper lawyer, who was a good friend of Desiree's, agreed to file a case, pro-bono, against the police for excessive force. After a few months, he dropped it, due to what he said was verbal harassment from my mother. She, apparently, in her grief, would leave him rambling messages about how the case wasn't progressing enough. And it ended.

I'm comforted that after decades of struggling with his anger and unhappiness, caused by a fatherless childhood in poverty, with no role models and few people who gave him attention, Derek is at peace, unable to lash out against himself or anyone else. The small, green, plastic alien now pokes out of the translucent bar of soap, which has evaporated over the years, as have my memories of the pain surrounding Derek. But, like the little alien still trapped inside, my complicated love for Derek will last the rest of my life.

FAMILY VALUABLES

When is it okay to tell people at a funeral that you're the deceased's secret illegitimate daughter? It was the first day of my dad's wake, and I did not know who knew about me. My husband, Randy, and I were heading into what felt like a real life soap opera, and we were forty-five minutes late. My cell phone rang.

"Jeneane?"

"Yes?"

"Where are you? We're all here waiting for you at the funeral home." About a dozen longtime friends were in the parking lot of the funeral home wondering where I was. The surprise relative had unknowingly brought a punctual entourage. What if someone asked them how they knew my dad?

"What? Oh, my gosh. We're stuck in traffic. And we need to change. We'll be there as soon as we can." I should have expected they would come to support me. Four days earlier, we were watching Transformers 2 together at a drive-in theater when my cell phone lit up with a Long Island number.

"Dad passed away about an hour ago. It was peaceful." My brother Sal said. "We're gonna finalize the arrangements tomorrow, but it looks like everything will be this weekend."

"Thank you, Sal," I said as my voice shook. "How're Joe and Mariana?" Joe was my other brother on my dad's side, and Mariana was my stepmother. They knew about me.

"They're praying. Please pray for him for the next seven nights so he can get into heaven. It's really important that you do so."

"Okay, I will, Sal. I'll see you this weekend. Thank you." I was grateful he called to let me know. They could have had the funeral and never told me about it to avoid revealing I existed. Randy watched as I sank into a profound, dark cry in the front seat of the car. We could hear Bumblebee saving the day on the drive-in movie radio signal. Randy turned off the sound, and we drove home.

"You know what grief is?" a colleague said to me once. "Grief is unexpressed love."

My dad's lung cancer spread to his bones before he even knew he had it. About eight months earlier, during one of our monthly calls, he explained. "I have to tell you something. I had some pain in my leg and they tried to do a bypass graph, but the pain wouldn't go away. Then, I had a scan, and I guess I have lung cancer that spread to my leg. They're gonna try some radiation. I wanted to let you know."

I was very worried. I knew my dad wasn't telling me how bad it was. He just wasn't a talker. During our monthly phone calls over the past thirteen or so years, we mostly chatted about unimportant things. I also knew about cancer and that he needed serious treatment. "You know, Sloan Kettering is the best place to go. Are you able to do that?"

"The doctors around here are pretty good. I'm gonna stick with them." I knew to leave it at that. It was important that he felt good about his care.

"Okay, Dad. Please let me know what is going on. I hope the treatment goes really well and you kick this thing."

It seemed like no time passed before I was visiting him in hospice. It was June. He was alert and appeared almost normal when I arrived, except for a raspy voice. He had an IV and was lying in his hospital bed. We talked a little bit about everything. "Why didn't you contact me when you were younger?" he asked.

"I had no idea where you were. I tried a bunch of things to find you but nothing worked."

"I'm sorry about all this. I asked your mom to marry me, but she said, 'No.'" He was opening up like never before. "Then she said she was marrying her new boyfriend, and I thought he would be your father and everything would be okay. I'm really sorry."

"Dad, I'm fine. There is nothing to be sorry about. Please don't feel bad or guilty," I said sincerely and emphatically. "I have everything I've ever wanted. I'm glad you were able to marry Mariana and have a happy life with Joe and Sal. My mother got a new boyfriend every two years. It would have been a nightmare for you."

The next time I saw my dad was six days before the funeral. He was barely conscious and on morphine. "Do you like turkey and Swiss cheese?" my brother Joe asked as we sat beside Dad's bed. My dad struggled to breathe in the background. Sal was there with his wife, Angelina, who was seven months pregnant, and their son Andrew, who was a little under two. Mariana was taking a break and would be back later.

"Yeah. Turkey and Swiss are my favorite." I said.

"Do you like mayonnaise?"

"Yeah"

"Well that's too bad because I don't have that." We laughed. "But, I'll nuke this and trust me, you'll love it." Joe handed me my favorite sandwich with no condiments and a Diet Orange Sunkist, which happened to be my favorite soda. I was happy that Joe seemed to have a sense of humor similar to mine. We caught up until the nurse came in and Angelina and I went out into the hall with Andrew.

"I don't feel good," Angelina said.

"Want me to hold Andrew?"

"Yes," and Angelina left the area.

I took my adorable nephew, who I had just met, and held him with his legs wrapped around my waist. He was perfectly silent and stared at me deeply with his big brown eyes, examining, judging. I sensed he could tell I had little motherly instinct. Sure, I took care of my younger sister, but that was decades ago. After about a minute, he snapped his head around and let out a short cry of disappointment, looking for his absent but competent mother. By the time she came back, my stepmother, Mariana, arrived, and I said goodbye to my dad for the last time.

Randy and I got to the funeral home about an hour and a half into Saturday's first wake, dressed in black suits. I couldn't imagine how it would go. My friends from upstate were waiting outside in flip flops and shorts...they had been on their way to Jones Beach. They said hello and followed us in. Sal, Joe, their wives, and Mariana were already there, as well as many other likely relatives. Mariana and my brothers greeted me, Randy, and my casually-dressed friends warmly. My dad lay in the coffin, pale, thin, and inanimate, with a rosary in his hands and his New York Giants swag. The smell of lilies filled the air. We paid our respects.

Pictures I had never seen before were displayed around the room, and I studied them closely. I thought, *How funny would it be if I Photoshopped myself into all of the family photos and just offered them up to Mariana and my brothers?* "Here, I fixed these," I would explain, waiting for a reaction. As I was looking at the photo board that thoughtfully included me and my father at my wedding, as well as pictures from my twenty-fifth birthday, a woman about my age walked up to me.

"How do you know my Uncle Bobby?" the woman asked.

"He was my father." I explained.

"What?" She asked in disbelief.

"I don't think he told many people, but he knew my mom before he met Mariana. I'm Jeneane. We're probably related." I held out my hand.

"I'm Andrea." She shook it. "My mother, Pearl, is his first cousin. I'm sorry, but I am in complete shock. How could he have kept that from us?"

"I don't really know. I didn't meet him until I was twenty-four. He did come to my wedding last year, though." I pointed to the picture of my dad and me at my wedding, somewhat as evidence. I was wearing a strapless, tea-length white dress and a veil. My dad wore a short-sleeved white shirt with a pocket protector. I had told him how much it would mean to me if he came to my wedding, and he showed up.

"Mariana couldn't make it. She gets car sick," he said as he arrived at my front door a couple of hours before the wedding.

"I'm so happy you came," I said hugging him. "You don't know how much it means to me." My fiancé, Randy, was already at our lake community lodge in upstate New York where our wedding would be taking place, setting up. It was a surprise wedding. We had been together for fourteen years and didn't want gifts or fuss. We staged my friend's surprise fortieth birthday party to get people to come on time, only telling the real story to close relatives who had to travel. The plan was for my father to bring me over to the lodge, where the rest of my family, including my mother, were helping to prepare.

"Would you like a tour of the house?" I asked my dad. I had designed the house plan and everything in it. I was excited to show him how I had realized my American dream. It had been a long road of hard work and risk taking.

"I need to be with someone with ambition," Randy explained during one of our breakups early on in our relationship. *What?* I thought. *You clearly do not know me.*

Fourteen years before our wedding, at twenty-three, Randy and

I met at work. He answered phones on the day shift, and I still worked nights, paying medical insurance claims--a holdover from going to morning and afternoon college classes. He would stay late and have dinner with me and our mutual friend Rhea in the cafeteria.

"This is how you build a sandwich that doesn't slip when you bite into it," I explained, showing the cross section of my turkey, Swiss, lettuce, tomato and mayonnaise sandwich. "You gotta keep the cheese away from the condiments and the tomato."

"Brilliant," Randy giggled. Randy was smart, funny, handsome, a little taller than I was, and fascinating. He looked like David Byrne, with dark, curly, unkempt hair, and he wore a red baseball cap at the office. Randy played guitar and piano and knew everything about midi multi-track recording. The best part was, he made his own computer cables.

I was single, in my own apartment, and happy. I went out to bars with friends but barely dated after the breakup with my first and only boyfriend, Will. It was hard for me to let men close after my mother's pattern of frequent man changes. Out of respect for myself, I flirted but didn't let people in. After a couple of unrequited crushes, which ended for me in heartbreak, I had stopped looking. I also learned my lesson: Never let a guy know you're interested because they like the chase.

One day after having regular, laughter-filled dinners with Randy, Rhea left a yellow Post-It note on my desk that simply read, "Randy." I picked it up and snickered. "No I'm not interested," I confessed and crumpled the note into the garbage. Secretly, I was though.

That day, my manager, Martha, called me into her office. "Why is Randy around your desk so much?" she inquired.

"I think he has a crush on me," I shared.

"Well, don't crush back," Martha sternly warned.

A couple of weeks later, I found myself at Randy's apartment on a Friday night with two other mutual friends. We had planned to watch Aladdin on Randy's big screen TV. I noticed his place was suspiciously clean, uncluttered, and orderly, atypical for upstate New York guys. *Maybe he isn't interested in women,* I wondered. Immediately, I darted to the bathroom. *He has to have hairballs in the shower,* I thought. And sure enough, I pulled back the curtain to see that there was a hair clump in the drain and two that had been pulled out and placed on the side of the tub so the water could escape. That's when I knew he was a possibility.

By the time of my first breakup with Randy, I had always known I would go to graduate school, but I wasn't sure for what. Law school? Higher education? Move to New York City and become a writer for David Letterman? Dreams were all I had, which was why I was incredulous at Randy's suggestion that I had no ambition. And sensing our pending breakup, I pre-spiked his glove compartment with a mean-looking Polaroid of myself, hoping he would find it later and miss me.

"You don't know what you're talking about. Do you know what I went through to get to this point? Leaving home at sixteen and putting myself through college? And, I'm going to get my master's, eventually. What do you have going on? What have you done in your life?" Randy was thirty-one and still finishing college, taking a single class per semester. He had come from a household with two parents who fed and clothed him.

After six weeks of our breakup, we missed each other and reunited. We laughed at the mean Polaroid. Still, I wasn't a hundred percent sure we would stay together, so when I left for NYU, I thought it would be over. But it wasn't. We saw each other on the weekends.

After NYU, I lived with Randy until I found a job near Albany as an instructional designer, and we moved to a rental on the lake where we live now. Our relationship got better and better. Randy went to graduate school, and we both worked hard in our careers to earn money, pay off student loans, and build our dream home.

Our house was constructed on a piece of waterfront property a few years before our wedding, and it was exactly what we wanted, contemporary with high ceilings, big windows, and hardwood floors. When I gave my father the tour on the day of the wedding, he seemed to struggle a bit to climb the stairs, but I didn't think anything of it. I was more concerned that my mother and father would be talking again for the first time in thirty-five years.

After my dad drove us to the lodge for the wedding, I reintroduced the two of them. My mom walked up, looked closely at my dad and said, "How *are* you?"

"I'm doing well. How are you?" They seemed to have good, light conversation. In that moment, I felt so fortunate to have both of my parents at my wedding. Randy's parents had passed. I introduced my dad to my sisters, Helene and Desiree, and her two kids, and my brother Edward, along with Randy's siblings and niece. The lodge overlooked the lake, and the room was set up audience-style so guests could roast the birthday boy. As the seats filled, the guests got into position and yelled, "Surprise" for my friend Jay.

My friend Krissy emceed the roast, asking audience members to share stories about the guest of honor. That's when Randy, my parents, and I slipped out and changed for the wedding. After the roast, Krissy handed the microphone to Jay and asked him to say a few words. He said, "Thanks for the surprise. Now I have a surprise for you," which signaled my nephew to play the wedding march. Randy walked out with the officiant. Then, my parents walked me out, and the room erupted in applause and tears as soon as they figured out the ruse.

Later on, after my father headed back to Long Island, my mother pulled me aside. "You know. Your father is a really nice guy."

"I know. Thanks for telling me that, Mom." *How bizarre,* I thought. *Aren't parents of a child supposed to know each other?*

A little over a year later, I was at my dad's funeral, explaining who I was.

"This is Dad's daughter, Jeneane," Joe said, introducing me to various cousins and friends.

"Your Bob Coppola's daughter? You're Bob Coppola's daughter? We're best friends thirty years and he never told us? I can't believe it," this lady said.

"Ma, you gotta meet her. This is Uncle Bobby's daughter." People continued to come up to me to introduce themselves. I sat with my husband toward the front of the room trying to process the commotion when an elderly gentleman walked over. He had a full head of neat gray hair parted on the side, glasses, a hearing aid, and a nicely fitting suit. He was my father's first cousin, more like his brother, since my dad was an only child. Sal and Joe called him Uncle Julie.

"You know, I knew about you, but I never said anything," he said, at what he thought was a lowered volume. "Bobby was spending a lot of time in Jackson Heights in the early seventies."

"Yeah, that's where we lived when I was a baby." A picture board with my dad's parents was close by.

"You know your grandmother and father kept company for eleven years before they got married," Uncle Julie said.

"Really? Randy and I were together for fourteen years before we got married. That's incredible!"

Uncle Julie walked back to his group of family members. "She seems nice!" he said with very loud voice, thinking he was whispering. Randy and I looked at each other and laughed.

The next few days were a blur—Joe's eulogy, three more wakes, meals, and the funeral with a Catholic mass on Monday. Randy stood by my side, talked and joked with new relatives, and supported me emotionally through it all. I longed for the relationship I should have had with my dad and his family. Why did he keep me a secret? Did he think he was protecting me somehow? And, why had I been so afraid to reach out to my brothers? I was nervous. I feared the family would eventually reject me and I would never see them again. I didn't want to end up with the type of estrangement my mother had so easily embraced.

A few weeks later, I received a large manila envelope in the mail. "I thought you would like to see this," my Uncle Julie wrote. Inside was a four-page family tree with my grandparents, father, step-mother, brothers, and many cousins. In a square connected to my dad's name, it said, "Jeneane." There were stories about my grand-parents in the package, along with a picture of the ship they took from Italy in the early 1900s. I was part of it. I belonged.

In July, Joe, his wife, Mia, and their two kids, Sophia and Anthony, will visit for the weekend, as they've done every July since my father passed. We'll go swimming, sing karaoke, make s'mores, and talk about upcoming events with the rest of the family. The kids will call us Aunt Jeneane and Uncle Randy, draw us pictures, and pick me wildflowers for my birthday.

I wish my dad were here to see that everything is okay. He prob-ably worried for thirty-nine years about keeping me a secret. I tried to show him I didn't need anything, but I did need one thing, family. In his death, he unknowingly left it to me. It's the best and most bittersweet gift my dad could have ever given.

AFTERWORD

While there's a lot more comedy and pain that didn't make this writing, we are all pretty well adjusted. Mom's retired and lives self-sufficiently in a small house in Casper, Wyoming. She's on oxygen, and manages to get around. She just renewed her motorcycle license. Her last boyfriend, Pogo, left after his insurance settlement came in, and she hasn't been with a man since. I send her peanut butter and jelly of the month, shoes with good arch support, and sometimes yeast.

Edward has a beautiful family in Casper and works in the energy field. Desiree was diagnosed with neuroendocrine tumors in 2001 and continues to battle her illness from Casper, where she is an office manager. She has two wonderful children and a grandson. Helene owns her own business outside of San Francisco, and Kenny retired from the Navy after serving honorably for thirty years, achieving the highest rank for an enlisted man.

Helene still visits her dad. Desiree, Edward, Derek, and Kenny's father's whereabouts are unknown. I was able to track down their cousins a few years ago, and they think he may have passed. He was seen strung out on drugs in the 1990s in Brooklyn. They have another half-sister. We keep in touch with some of the cousins via Facebook.

I try to see Joe, Sal, Mariana, and the extended Coppola family as much as I can.

I have a fulfilling job managing a national team of instructional designers and visit Wyoming at least once a year, when there is no pandemic. We laugh and joke about the silliness of the past, eat bad food, and drink foo-foo cocktails.

If I could freeze the day of this writing, I would, because life is as good as it will ever be.

ACKNOWLEDGEMENT

I want to thank Tom Curran, Jackie Rogers, Roberta Wilson, and "Babs" Linda Lou for supporting and encouraging me to write these stories.

You are all talented beyond words.

ABOUT THE AUTHOR

J. Walker

Against the odds, Jeneane Walker is an American success story. Born as the fifth of six children to a single mother in Queens, New York, and raised by poodles on welfare and food stamps, she left home at sixteen to pursue higher education. After earning an M.A. in Educational Communication and Technology from NYU, and learning how to create corporate training videos and online tutorials, she faked her way into the field of instructional design.

Now, with thirty years at her current company, and no more student loans, she is the Director of a top notch national instructional design team. Jeneane lives with her husband, Randy, on a lake in upstate New York. She loves to laugh, brew beer, sing karaoke, drink cocktails, and write about the bizarre past most people choose to forget.

www.ingramcontent.com/pod-product-compliance
Lightning Source LLC
Chambersburg PA
CBHW060941040426

42445CB00011B/956